# BRITISH MUNICIPAL BUSES IN PORTUGAL

DAVID HARVEY

AMBERLEY

*Front cover*: Working on the 3 route in Lisbon's Praça do Comércio in September 1978 is 309 (BD-42-09). One of the later AEC Regent V D2LAs of the first batch, 309 was delivered in September 1957. Like all the rear-entrance buses, it arrived with a Weymann H32/26R seating layout, which was increased to H37/28R bodywork in June 1966. 309 is in the green and white Carris livery and was withdrawn in November 1979. (PM Photography)

*Back cover*: The driver of 332 (SN-72-12) prepares to leave the Praça de Bandeira, Oporto, when working on the 78 route in August 1984. The sign that would be displayed beneath the nearside windscreen to indicate that it was being one-man-operated is not there, which is confirmed by the conductor standing on the platform. 332 entered service in October 1987 and was later saved for preservation by STCP. (D. R. Harvey)

First published 2019

Amberley Publishing
The Hill, Stroud
Gloucestershire, GL5 4EP

www.amberley-books.com

British Library Cataloguing in Publication Data.
A catalogue record for this book is available from the British Library.

ISBN 978 1 4456 9263 0 (print)
ISBN 978 1 4456 9264 7 (ebook)

Typeset in 10pt on 13pt Sabon.
Typesetting by Aura Technology and Software Services, India.
Printed in the UK.

# Contents

# Introduction

Recently married and looking for somewhere to go on holiday, my wife and I decided to go to the Algarve in southern Portugal in 1981, with the prospect of sun, sand, a splendid cuisine and an abundance of beer and wine. At that time the area had not developed its identity and was a mixture of luxury hotels (which were too expensive!), emerging golf courses (we couldn't play golf!), 18–30 type holidays (we were on the cusp!) and a lively very late night life (which neither of us wanted!). The result was that after a week we decided to escape and go on a four-day trip to Lisbon and that began a love affair with the capital and the north of Portugal that lasted over several holidays for the next ten years.

One of the outcomes of these holidays was a huge cache of tram, bus and trolleybus photographs taking in most of the larger cities of the country. This was at the time when British buses were beginning to wane as they were coming towards the end of their lives and were being rapidly being replaced by European manufacturers' products built by MAN, Mercedes-Benz, Scania and Volvo. Left-hand drive 'mirror-image' half-cab double-deck buses were still operating in Lisbon and Oporto while rear-engined double-deckers of the 1960s mingled with trams, trolleybuses and newer Continental single-deckers. Our first visits to the larger urban centres showed a vehicle situation that had not changed in perhaps twelve years, but within the next decade the change was almost complete and the half-cab double and single-deckers had all but gone.

Now, nearly forty years later, I have used many of the stock of photographs I took then as a basis for this book. This book does not examine the many independent bus and coach operators, or the former Rodoviária Nacional (RN), Portugal's national bus company. At this distance in time there might be some errors in exact locations but hopefully this will be forgiven in this look back into the Portuguese past when British-built buses were in abundance in the larger urban areas.

# British Buses in Portugal

For many, Portugal is a country suited for tourism, with a hot summer climate influenced by the west-facing Atlantic climate. Long sandy beaches dominate the country and the Algarve and Atlantic coast attract sun-seekers from all over Europe, but there is much more to Portugal. The Tagus and Douro valleys contain some of the most spectacular scenery in Iberia with the mild Atlantic Mediterranean climate enabling the landscape to remain green throughout the year. Small market towns and picturesque villages abound and yet most of inland Portugal is within a two to three-hour drive of the sea.

Historically, Portugal has been Britain's oldest ally, with the Anglo-Portuguese alliance ratified at the Treaty of Windsor in 1386. Throughout the country magnificent architectural gems exist, many dating from the time when Portugal was one of the most economically powerful countries in Europe. Its wealth came after the fifteenth century, from the exploration of South America, Africa and South East Asia trading in spices. From the seventeenth century Portugal became a powerful trading nation with many colonies supplying minerals and agricultural products while Portugal exported copper, cork and many agricultural products including wines and particularly the British-developed port wine industry from the River Douro area based around Oporto and Vila Nova de Gaia. Since the revolution of 1974 a considerable amount of new industry has been developed in Portugal. Industry is diversified, including numerous multi-national car manufacturers such as Volkswagen and Peugeot-Citroën, aerospace firms Embraer and OGMA, as well as electronics and textiles.

Portugal is a relatively small country with a population of around 11 million that for many years was controlled by the Estado Novo (Second Republic) Party, which to some extent caused the country to become one of the poorest in Western Europe. Prior to the 1990s, Portugal had the look of a country with a faded grandeur, a large number of historic and architectural charms in the towns and cities, but appearing 'unfinished' with roads, bridges and urban renewal seemingly being started but often incomplete. After joining the then EEC in 1986, economic restructuring and investment have made the country far more prosperous, but in return this has made the country more anonymously European.

For many years, Portugal was a country whose transport systems were dominated by British influence. Many of the tram fleets were owned and financed by British companies, but this was largely concealed by the designs of the tramcars and their electrical equipment. The larger municipal operators, such as Lisbon and Oporto, all subscribed to British-built buses, with AEC being the dominant exporter to Portugal. Mule-hauled trams were introduced in Lisbon in 1872 and after the first tram electrification schemes in the early 1900s, trams were virtually the only form of urban public transport until immediately after the Second World War when buses were introduced, initially all single-deckers but after 1950 'mirror-image' British-styled double-deckers began to be delivered. New trolleybus systems were opened in Coimbra (1947), Oporto (1959) and Braga (1961). These are outside the remit for this volume, but in both Coimbra and Oporto many of the trolleybus chassis were of British manufacture.

**24 (BI-15-47)**
One of the Dalfa-bodied Daimler CVD6s of 1949, 24 (BI-15-47), in the 1960 turquoise and ivory livery, speeds over the tram tracks and cobbles, which no doubt contributed to these bodies being replaced after some eighteen years, although even the new bodies only lasted until 1975. These buses were known for their smooth running Daimler CD6 8.6 litre engines, but subsequent orders for buses gradually moved away from Daimlers as the CD6 unit tended to burn engine oil. (D. R. Harvey Collection)

# The Municipal Operators of British Buses

## A. Lisbon

Lisbon, the capital of Portugal and dating as a settlement from pre-Roman times, slopes up from the broad River Tagus valley on to some seven hills. By the mid-eighteenth century, Lisbon had become one of the largest cities and trading ports in Europe. On 1 November 1755, during the reign of King Dom José I, there was a powerful earthquake registering an estimated 8.5 on the Richter Scale followed by a 40-foot-high tsunami. Lisbon was consumed by fire and after a week of burning 90 per cent of the city had been destroyed, with a maximum estimated death toll of 100,000 people. It is still one of Europe's worst natural disasters and left a deep impression on Portugal's collective psyche, often heard of today in the traditional Fado folksongs.

After the 1755 earthquake, the city was rebuilt largely according to the plans of the Prime Minister, the 1st Marquess of Pombal. The lower town began to be known as the Baixa Pombalina. Instead of rebuilding the medieval town, Pombal decided to demolish what remained after the earthquake and rebuild the city centre in accordance with principles of modern urban design. The rebuilt city centre was built in a renaissance style with broad streets built on a grid pattern. It was reconstructed in an open rectangular plan with two great squares with elegant buildings, open squares and broad avenues including the Praça do Rossio, Praça do Figueira and the Praça do Comércio, the latter covering the site of Ribeira Palace. The first and second of these squares are in the central commercial district, the traditional gathering places of the city and the location of the older cafés, theatres and restaurants; the second became the city's main access to the River Tagus and the point of departure and arrival for seagoing vessels, adorned by a triumphal arch (1873) and monument to King Joseph I. Lisbon still retains much of its eighteenth-century architectural grandeur. The part of the city that survived the earthquake is the Alfama district, a warren of apparently impenetrable lanes and alleys built on the steep hills just inland from the River Tagus. The trams do succeed in penetrating the Alfama, on the route 28, which is one of the great tram rides of the world.

Companhia Carris de Ferro de Lisboa (CCFL), to give it its full title, is Lisbon's municipal operator. It operates its trams on a narrow 3-ft gauge with a maximum fleet strength of around 300 trams, three funicular railways and a lift and a metro system opened in 1959 as well as a bus fleet of around 800 vehicles. Carris was originally a British-owned company, Lisbon Electric Tramways, that electrified the original mule tramway to Belem in 1901. Tram operation with both bogie and four-wheeled tramcars dominated Lisbon until the late 1930s with routes along the River Tagus valley beyond Belem to Alges and Estadio downstream and to Poco Do Bispo upstream. Long services inland to the north reached Benfica, Luz and Lumiar but these were replaced by the Metro system. The Lisbon Metro has four lines running on 26.8 miles of route and with fifty-five stations.

In 1958 the old Lisbon tramway network had comprised some thirty-eight routes, but it been largely taken out of central Lisbon following the opening of the Lisbon Metro in December 1959 and it had been announced in 1972 that the trams would be phased out altogether, but in 1978 it was decided that the trams would be retained and rebuilt for the River Tagus riverside and hilly routes.

In 2019, there are just six tram routes in operation, compared to the thirty-nine in 1957. Surviving routes include the amazingly hilly and twisting Graça Circle 28 route. It runs from São Tome down into the Baixa in the commercial heart of the city and then uphill to the Bairro Alto on top of another of Lisbon's hills. Four-wheel rebuilt trams run on this service as well as the 12 route from Praça da Figueira to São Tome, while a fleet of preserved museum tramcars operates for the tourists. Alongside the River Tagus is the 15 route to Belém and Alges, which was the domain of large bogie cars dating from between 1903 and 1906 and numbered 283–362. Later bogie cars used on this route included 801–810, built between 1939 and 1943, which had domed roofs and flush side panels, and ten modern-looking bogie cars built in 1947 and numbered 901–910. Subsequent developments in Lisbon saw the replacement in 1995 of these large bogie trams with the introduction of modern tramcars: ten Siemens-built articulated trams, numbered 501–510, for use on the 15 route. A further ten cars were ordered in 2018 for this long and most attractive service alongside the River Tagus to Belem, Algés and beyond.

Motor bus operation by Carris began in June 1912 with five cross-bench twenty-one-seat Leyland Xs, followed by a pair of Tilling-Stevens TS3s and three small Austin 20 hp buses in 1914. All had been withdrawn by 1917. Buses were not to be seen again on the streets of Lisbon until 1939 when six full-sized buses were purchased. CCFL bought this small fleet of single-deck AEC Regent 0661s for the 1940 Portuguese World Exhibition at Belem. Unfortunately they had to be all stored until the end of the war as due to the international situation the event was cancelled. They were right-hand drive buses with Weymann bodies and lasted until 1968.

After the end of the Second World War, although trams continued to be built between 1947 and 1963, the British bus connection continued when CCFL tried out penny numbers of Leyland Titan PD1 double-deckers and Maudslay Marathon and Albion Valkyrie single-deckers, all with right-hand drive. These were soon followed between 1946 and 1950 by 100 new AEC Regals, mostly left-hand drive with either Weymann or Saunders bodies, as well as small batches of Daimler CVUs, which were really badge-engineered Guy Victorys. Between 1950 and 1967, 110 AEC Regent IIIs and 256 Regent Vs were purchased by Lisbon, all with either British-built or styled Weymann bodies which, with their left-hand drive half-cabs and right-hand open rear platforms, were a mirror image of buses operating in the United Kingdom.

In 1966 the Carris name was adopted on the vehicles and with the new identity the old, very British livery of predominantly green was replaced by a more gaudy orange and off-white livery echoed by SELNEC in Manchester in 1969. The last Regent Vs were forward-entrance buses, with UTIC-built bodies made to Weymann designs. Fifty left-hand drive Daimler Fleetline CRG6LXs with CCFL-built bodies made in a style resembling Weymann bodywork were built between 1967 and 1969 while five more Fleetlines with much squarer-designed UTIC dual-door bodies entered service in 1971.

The Portuguese 'Carnation' Revolution overthrew the Marcelo Caetano Premiership on 25 April 1974 and over a million Portuguese ex-pats returned to mainland Portugal. It was necessary to press every tram and bus into service, giving many old British buses a new lease of life.

From 1973 the winds of change had blown the British bus connection completely out of the water. The British bus industry was in crisis due in part to the Three-Day Week policy of the Edward Heath Conservative government. British Leyland had bought up, taken over and subsequently closed down many production plants, leaving it with chassis that had been inherited from formerly independent bus manufacturers, such as Bristol, Daimler and Leyland. These were chassis that had been in production for up to fifteen years, and while having been upgraded, they were often 'last year's' models. They were expensive to purchase and were rapidly being overtaken in terms of performance, technological equipment and purchase price by Continental rivals. There was also the mentality that if it was British it had to be better than "foreign stuff", which was rapidly proving not to be the case.

On 21 December 1973 a decree came into effect stating that the leasing contract of Lisbon Electric Tramways Ltd should be rescinded and a new concession for all modes was made for fifty years with Carris. The municipality bought 67 per cent of CCFL's shares and on 1 January 1974 Lisbon Electric Tramways Ltd changed its identity to LET (Holdings) Ltd. As a result any ties with former British owners came to an end and with no suitable British single-decker chassis available, save for the possibility of purchasing Leyland Nationals. From 1975 MAN, Mercedes-Benz, Iveco and Volvo were bought in very large numbers, resulting in the elimination of virtually all the British-built chassis in Lisbon by the mid-1990s. The result was that Lisbon's bus fleet soon lost its individualistic appearance and took on a blandly European appearance, a trend which soon occurred in all of Portugal's municipal bus fleets. Further new investment came when a new bus garage at Pontinha replaced the Amoreiras bus garage on 1 October 1976.

The British buses in the CCFL fleet disappeared quite rapidly, beginning in the early 1980s with the final AEC Regal IIIs and Regent Vs going in 1991. The last all-day Regal III route was service 13A (Praça do Comércio – Chélas) from Miraflores Garage, being replaced by Ivecos in 1987, while the last Regent V route was service 39 (Praça São Bento – Marvila) from Pontinha Garage. The last Regal IIIs in service were 110 and 117, working out their lives on assorted peak-hour extras.

The last Daimler Fleetlines were extensively used on the Linha Verde (Green Line) 90 service to Lisbon Airport in the 1980s. They were regularly seen on service 81 (Praça do Comércio – Rotunda Encarnacao) from Cabo Ruivo depot, but latterly operated the 57 (Marques de Pombal – Chelas) on Monday to Friday peak hours until they were finally taken out of service during the summer of 1995.

# 1. Half-Cab Single-Deckers

### 1 (HB-11-11)
*Above*: The first British buses to be purchased by CCFL were six AEC Regent 0661 which had Weymann B32D bodywork. They had a 16 ft 3 in. wheelbase and an AEC 7.58-litre engine which left them somewhat underpowered on the steep hills of Lisbon. The first of these right-hand drive single-deckers mounted on a double-decker body was 1 (HB-11-11), seen parked in Santo Amaro tram depot yard in 1940. (CCFL)

### 1-6
*Opposite Above*: The first batch of six single-deckers are lined up in the garage yard in 1940 when newly delivered. On the left is 4 (EL-11-11) with 3 (AE-11-13) and 5 (ED-11-11) beyond. These right-hand drive single-deckers were built in 1939 for the 1940 Portuguese World Exhibition at Belem. Unfortunately, they were all stored until the end of the Second World War as the event was cancelled because of the international situation. These buses had long lives and lasted until 1968. (CCFL)

**2 (GA-11-09)**

*Below*: After being in store from new in 1940, the six AEC Regent 0661s with attractive Weymann B32D bodies were placed into service in 1946. They were right-hand drive and from the British nearside looked similar to the six AEC Regal 0662s, also with Weymann bodywork, that were supplied to Liverpool Corporation as FKB 361–366 in the two months after the outbreak of the Second World War in 1939. 2 (GA-11-09) crosses the Avenida da Liberdade during the late 1950s while in the distance an Austin A105 Westminster taxi pulls across the dual carriageway. (PM Photography)

## 7 (DE-12-61)

*Above*: Passing Arco de Cego tram depot on 22 July 1967 is the first of the post-war buses delivered to Lisbon. This occurred in January 1947 and they were right-hand drive AEC Regal II 0662 chassis with Weymann metal-framed B32D bodywork. The bodywork had deep louvered guttering above the saloon's deep windows which, coupled to the substantial steel bumper bar, gave them a very Continental appearance. The tumblehome on the lower panels by contrast was a very British contemporary design feature. (A. D. Packer)

## 9 (EI-12-34)

*Below*: 9 (EI-12-34), one of the six right-hand drive Weymann-bodied AEC Regal II 0662s delivered in January 1947. It had an extra bay and at 30 ft long was longer than the previous buses, which had the export 19 ft 0 in. wheelbase. These buses had AEC A173 7.58-litre engines coupled to a four-speed constant mesh manual gearbox. It is working on the 18 route to Alcântara on 22 July 1967 and stands in Largo do Rato, to the north of the city centre, alongside the castellated stone wall in the centre of the square next to the bus stop. (A. D. Packer)

**10 (AG-12-37)**
*Above*: The earliest post-war single-deckers delivered to Lisbon were another six AECs which looked very similar to the 1939 Regents, but were Regal II 0662s with a longer wheelbase of 17 ft 6 in. and were fitted with AEC 7.58-litre engines. The six had similar-looking Weymann B32D bodywork and still had right-hand drive chassis. 10 (AG-12-37) entered service in November 1946 and stands at the Alcântara terminus in the late 1960s. These six buses, numbered 7–12, had the very first post-war AEC Regal II 0662 chassis numbers, with 10 being the third one, numbered 06624003. This was the last of the half-dozen buses of the 7–12 class and survived until July 1970. (A. Phillips)

**126 (CF-12-89)**
*Below*: Lisbon's first batch of Leyland Tiger OPS1s was numbered 125–128 and had Cinco Irmâos Ŭnidos B32D bodywork, which was of composite construction and somewhat frail; as a result these OPS1s were rebodied with second-hand Saunders bodies removed from slightly newer AEC Regal IIIs, which had a half-cab structure which seems slightly at odds with the rest of the front profile. Fitted with this second hand body, 126 (CF-12-89) travels towards Praça do Comércio from Praça da Figueira in Rua da Prata in the Baixa. (A. D. Packer)

**130 (GB-14-14) and 129 (GB-14-16)**
*Above*: In April 1947, a pair of CCFL-bodied right-hand drive Leyland Tiger PS1s, numbered 129 and 130, were delivered and entered service in December 1948, having taken over twenty months to be bodied by the operator. When compared to the contemporary AEC Regal IIIs, the Leylands, including four slightly earlier ones with Cinco Irmâos Ŭnuidos B32D bodies, were not so suitable for the hills in Lisbon. They had the Leyland E181 7.4-litre engine coupled to a constant mesh gearbox mounted on a chassis with a 17 ft 6 in. wheelbase. While the CIŬ bodies required replacement as early as 1952, this pair were both sold to Nazaré in April 1963, where 130 lasted until 1967. 129 survived slightly longer, until April 1968, on the short, fearsome climb from Praia, the old fishing village on the beach, to the cliff-top villages of Sítio and Pederneira. (D. R. Harvey Collection)

**133 (EB-12-57)**
*Opposite above*: Just three AEC Regal II 0662s were equipped with bodies by local coachbuilder Stand Moderno with a rather attractive B32D layout. This was typical of the urgent requirements of CCFL to get chassis bodied and into service as quickly as possible. The original composite body was soon replaced with a B32D body by CCFL in April 1954. The middle one of the three, 133 (EB-12-57), was a right-hand drive chassis and entered service in January 1947. The bus is crossing the Avenida da Liberdade on 14 July 1964. (A. D. Packer)

### 135 (BI-13-61)

*Below*: Standing at Lisbon Airport is a Russo-bodied Albion Valkyrie CX13, 135 (BI-13-61). This was the first of a quintet of these chassis, with 135 entering service in July 1948. Although the Albion chassis was an extremely robust one, the attractively proportioned Russo bodies were not and all four were rebodied by CCFL with B32D bodywork as early as 1952. They all lasted until the mid-1960s. In the year after the end of the Second World War, bus operators throughout Portugal were quite desperate to acquire new stock. The country's historical links to the United Kingdom, plus the British Labour Party's urgent requirement to export everything and anything because of the near bankrupt state of the country, meant that buses built for the Iberian Peninsula, the Middle East and South America, where the rule of the road was on the right, were supplied as normal British right-hand drive vehicles, thus the layout of this Albion Valkyrie and other contemporary late 1940s imports. (A. Johnson)

## 141 (EC-12-96)

*Above*: Parked in Amoreiras Garage yard on 23 July 1964 is right-hand drive 141 (EC-12-96), a Maudslay Marathon III that had been rebodied with a four-year-old Weymann B32D body in 1951. The Marathon III chassis was not normally bodied as a bus though quite a number of them were exported to Portugal; with the exception of Lisbon's four, they were usually bodied as coaches. After Maudslay was taken over by ACV in March 1948, the petrol-engined Mark II model was quietly dropped and subsequently all Marathon IIIs were fitted with AEC 7.57-litre diesel engines. (A. D. Packer)

## 15 (FB-13-95)

*Below*: Parked at the Alcântara terminus between the River Tagus Estuary and the overlooking hills in April 1967 is 15 (FB-13-95). This AEC Regal III 0963 was one of the first batch of this model, numbered 13–22, which were for the first time left-hand drive vehicles. All four had Weymann B24D bodywork finished off by CCFL's workshops. 15 entered service in April 1948 and benefitted from having the larger 9.6-litre engine, which could cope better with the hills of Lisbon. In this form, 15 survived until 1969. It was then renumbered 140 and fitted with a new B32D body, surviving until July 1986. (R. Symons)

**23 (?)**

*Above*: The identity of this bus is something of a mystery. It lacks a Portuguese number plate and carries the fleet number 73, which was a similar left-hand drive Regal III but with a Saunders B24D body. This AEC Regal III 0963 is still at Weymann's factory in Addlestone prior to delivery in 1948. It might be 23 (IL-14-50), which was the first of CCFL's Regals to be bodied completely by Weymann. It has a Weymann dual-door twenty-four-seater body with room for a large number of standing passengers. The bus has the characteristic curved cab window in front of the driver's door, while the rather square rear profile of the bus is to allow more headroom for the passengers in the standee area behind the rear axle. Soon this bus would be driven to Newport docks in South Wales for dispatch by ship to Lisbon. (Weymann)

**33 (BG-13-99)**

*Below*: The first left-hand drive buses to be delivered to Carris were AEC Regal III 0963s numbered 13–54, which arrived between March and December 1948. 33 (BG-13-99) had the usual style of Weymann B24D bodywork with room for as many standing passengers as could be crammed in. Later renumbered 124 and fitted with a CCFL B15D body, 33 enters the Praça do Comércio on 24 July 1967, just about twelve months before it received its new standee-style body. (A. D. Packer)

## 51 (LF-14-29)

*Above*: The terminus of the 42 route was at Alcântara. Located to the west of Lisbon, Alcântara grew up near to the Roman bridging point of the River Tagus. In the nineteenth century the area developed as a downstream industrial port for Lisbon, though in the latter part of the twentieth century, as the area declined, so the former warehouses became gentrified and the area became a centre for Lisbon's nightlife. Long before all that, on 24 July 1967, 51 (LF-14-29), an AEC Regal III 0963 still sporting its original Weymann B24D body, is parked next to the Alcântara Terra railway station awaiting its next duty. After rebodying in 1969, this bus was renumbered 146. (A. D. Packer)

## 58 (IF-13-42)

*Below*: Saunders of Beaumaris, Anglesey, supplied Lisbon with sixty bodies mounted on AEC Regal III 0963 chassis. These had the large AEC A207 9.6-litre oil engine and pre-selector gearboxes. A well-loaded 58 (IF-13-42), overlooked by balconied and shuttered four-storey residences, is working on the short 9 route to Campo de Ourique, just to the west of the city centre, in 1957 and stands in the Praça da Figueira. The bus was rebodied by UTIC as a front-entrance double-decker in February 1967 and was renumbered 442. In this guise it was not withdrawn until February 1978. (R. F. Mack)

### 66 (IA-13-82)

*Above*: Waiting to be taken away from Beaumaris for export in March 1948 is 66 (IA-13-82), one of the AEC Regal III 0963s for Lisbon. Close inspection shows the details of the finished bus such as the handles on the front entrance and rear exit sliding doors. Another nice touch is the aluminium spill plate below the fuel filler cap between the doors. The advertisements in the windows proclaim that the coachwork is built by SEAS, the company name for Saunders Engineering & Shipyard Ltd. (SEAS)

### 91 (FA-15-02)

*Below*: With the driver and conductor having a welcome break at the back of the saloon in the Praça do Comércio. 91 (FA-15-02) is parked in the city centre, having worked in from Benfica on the 15 route. There were sixty AEC Regal III 0963s built by Saunders, which had rather plain-looking 8-foot-wide bodywork with rear entrance and front exit sliding doors. They had seating for twenty-four passengers and a further twenty-one standees. Their appearance was not helped by the deep sunshade with ventilated louvres over the almost square-shaped saloon windows, as well as a square front profile with a straight bottom to the driver's windscreen. 91 would be rebodied by UTIC with a double-deck sixty-five-seater body with a forward entrance and be renumbered 469. (PM Photography)

**108 (ex-60) (IA-13-39)**
*Above*: The conductor appears to be encouraging the driver to keep the bus going as the AEC Regal III works up a steep hill over the cobbled street. This is 108 (ex-60) (IA-13-39). It is on the 13 service to Serafina parkland area to the west of the city. 108 was originally fitted with a Saunders B24D framed body completed by CCFL and entered service in March 1950. It was rebodied by UTIC with a B15 plus standees in 1972 and then pounded the hills of Lisbon until it was withdrawn in 1986. (D. R. Harvey Collection)

**111 (ex-45) (EB-14-31) and 114 (ex-44) (CI-14-08)**
*Below*: Parked in Miraflores garage yard in August 1988 are 111 (ex-45) (EB-14-31) and 114 (ex-44) (CI-14-08). These rebodied AEC Regal III 9631Es had both been rebodied by CCFL in November and December 1970 with five-bay bodywork and a two-door layout but with a small window behind the rear door. Both would remain in service until the early 1990s as crew-operated buses as neither vehicle had been rebuilt with a nearside cab diagonal window. (D. R. Harvey)

## 116 (ex-42) (CI-14-06)

*Above*: Passing through the Praça do Comércio in August 1985 is AEC Regal III 9631E 116 (ex-42) (CI-14-06). The body on this bus was rebodied by CCFL as late as December 1981 to the larger thirty-two-seat capacity with a single-width rear door and a larger rear side window than those that were operated with a seated conductor. Also known as Terreiro do Paço or 'The Palace's Square', the Praça do Comércio is a large, rectangular square in the shape of a U, open towards the River Tagus, begun to replace the destruction of Lisbon after the 1755 earthquake. The new Praça do Comércio was filled with government bureaux regulating customs and port activities. The grand eighteenth-century symmetrical lemon-coloured buildings have arcades and shops on the ground floor. On the north side of the square's mosaic cobbles pavements is a triumphal arch, in front of which stands 116 (CI-14-06). (D. R. Harvey)

## 123 (ex-54) (FL-14-06)

*Below*: AEC Regal III 9631E 123 (ex 54) (FL-14-06) entered service in February 1949 with a Weymann B24D body. It was rebuilt in December 1967 by CCFL using the original Weymann frames. It had a wide double rear door, allowing for a seated conductor, which with the added space for standee passengers resulted in a low B16D seating capacity. It was withdrawn exactly twenty years later and was sold to the Oxford Bus Museum. It is seen negotiating a tight right turn on the steep hills found on the 37 São Tome service. (D. R. Harvey Collection)

## 132 (ex-35) (BG-14-00)

*Above*: Formerly numbered 35 and having a Weymann/CCFL B15D body, 132 (BG-14-00) is parked alongside the outer stone wall of Lisbon's St George Castle. São Jorge Castle is a Moorish castle built in the mid-eleventh century on the site of a sixth-century fortress. It occupies a commanding hilltop overlooking Lisbon's city centre and the River Tagus. The original castle walls are made of granite and have a roughly square plan with an outer motte wall forming an encircling citadel, which is where this AEC Regal III 9631E is parked. This fortified castle is situated in the area most difficult to access at the top of the hill, making use of the natural, easily defended slopes to the north and west. São Jorge Castle was not meant as a residence but was built to house troops and, in case of siege, had eleven tall defensive towers. (PM Photography)

## 142 (ex 16) (IA-13-82)

*Below*: The Marques de Pombal roundabout is located between the Avenida da Liberdade and the Eduardo VII Park to the north of the main shopping area in Lisbon's city centre. AEC Regal III 9631E 142 (ex-16) (IA-13-82) is being overtaken by an Opel Viva saloon. The well-loaded 142 started its long life in April 1948. It was rebodied by CCFL using the original Weymann bodywork framing in 1969 and continued to operate in the green livery with a white-painted waistrail until the mid-1970s. 142 remained in service until December 1990. (D. R. Harvey Collection)

# 2. Half-Cab Exposed Radiator Double-Deckers

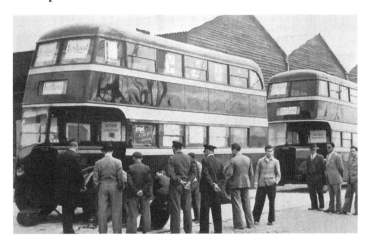

### 201 (II-13-09) and 202 (HL-13-11)

*Above*: The need for something with a greater seating capacity than the single-decker fleet encouraged CCFL to again look to British bus manufacturers. The first pair of double-deckers to enter service in Lisbon was 201 and 202 which both entered service in June 1947. These were Leyland Titan PD1As with Leyland E181 7.4-litre engines and bodies built by Lancashire Aircraft who only built ten of these Leyland-style bodies under licence; the other eight went to Douglas Corporation. They are being inspected in May 1947 by senior management staff and mechanics before entry into service in Santo Amaro tram yard. A kind of tutorial seems to be taking place on how to change a front wheel! (CCFL)

### 202 (HL-13-11)

*Below*: The only slightly continental feature on the pair of otherwise British-looking Leyland Titan PD1A buses, was that rubber bushes sourced from Metalastic Ltd were used in place of copper bushes in the spring shackles was that they were retrospectively fitted with a substantial steel bumper across the bottom of the front wings. 202 (HL-13-11), had a H30/26R seating layout and were the only double-deckers ever operated with a right hand drive layout and still looks remarkably smart as it works on the Moscavide route in 1963 when it was nearly sixteen years old. It was finally withdrawn in 1973. (A. Johnson)

## 204 (EF-16-79)

*Above*: Leaving Sete Rios on 21 July 1964 is 204 (EF-16-79). This was the second of the initial batch of six AEC Regent III 9631Es which entered service in November and December 1950. They had like the contemporary Regal IIIs, a four-speed fluid flywheel preselector gearbox coupled to the AEC A207 9.6 litre engine which made the life of the driver much easier than buses fitted with a crash gearbox. This Weymann-bodied AEC Regent III 9631E is still in the livery of the double-deck fleet as introduced in 1950 with the white roof and upper saloon window surrounds. It still has its roof mounted front side lights and the large unpainted fender across the bottom of the front wings and the radiator. (A. D. Packer)

## 205 (DB-16-97)

*Below*: Loading up passengers on the eastern side of the Praça Dom Pedro IV, better known locally as Rossio Square, in August 1981 is 205 (DB-16-97), one of the first left-hand drive AEC Regent III 9631E double-deckers. It had entered service in December 1950 as one of a trial batch of six buses with this very British-looking Weymann H30/26R bodywork, which proved to be the model adopted by CCFL for the next six years. 205 was twice reseated and ran for the last fifteen years in service with a H37/28R seating layout. The buildings in Rossio to the left of the bus are lined with cafés, bars and restaurants and this is one of Lisbon's most splendid and famous squares. (D. R. Harvey)

### 209 (IG-18-10)

*Above*: Standing in Rossio Square on 16 July 1964 is AEC Regent III 9631E 209 (IG-18-10). The Weymann body, even when over thirteen years old, still retains its white-painted roof, its cantrail gutter strips and, unusually, a set of side lights set into the front dome. Adorned with the advertisement for Dunlop tyres, beside the fact that it is left-hand drive, the bus looks as though it should be operating in a provincial British town rather than the capital of Portugal. (A. D. Packer)

### 211 (IG-18-12)

*Below*: The mirror image of a typical British double-decker is well illustrated by 211 (IG-18-12) as it waits for more passengers in the Praça do Comércio in the summer of 1957. This fifty-six-seater Weymann-bodied exposed radiator AEC Regent III 9631E entered service in December 1951 as part of a group numbered 209–246. The bus is carrying an advertisement for the famous Café Nicola, originally opened in the late eighteenth century. This famous Lisbon café originally opened in the late eighteenth century. In 1929, Nicola moved to its current location in the Praça Dom Pedro IV and features a splendid art deco frontage. (R. F. Mack)

### 213 (GH-18-11)

*Above*: Parked on the typical cobbled street outside a suburban jeweller's shop, well hidden from the strong summer sunlight by the canvas shop blind, is an AEC Regent III 9631E with a Weymann H30/26R body. 213 (GH-18-11) is working on the 16 route back to Cais do Sodré, its railway station and the suburban line to Estoril and Cascais in 1964. The woman in the Portuguese long dress carries her heavy bundle on her head in the traditional way that was perhaps more common in rural towns and coastal villages. Behind the bus, the rows of washing hanging on the balconies, so typical of the older areas of Lisbon, will quickly dry in the hot weather. (R. F. Mack)

### 217 (IF-18-17)

*Opposite above*: Standing over the pits in the workshops of Miraflores Garage in August 1988 is the Carris-preserved AEC Regent III left-hand drive bus. The mirror-image Weymann H30/26R body entered service in February 1952 and after a hard life of thirty-one years pounding the cobbled streets of Lisbon, it was saved for preservation in January 1983. Restored to its original green and white livery, the bus was stripped back to its metal frames and rebuilt with new panels. The original rear destination box was restored while the rear platform and staircase were virtually new structures. It really did look magnificent! (D. R. Harvey)

### 220 (BD-18-47)

*Opposite below*: Standing in the Praça Dom Pedro IV Square in September 1978 is 220 (BD-18-47). Entering service in May 1952, this AEC Regent III 9631E was to stay in use until March 1980, which by comparison to a contemporary UK-based Weymann-bodied Regent III combination was well over double the service life in considerably more extreme climatic and geographical conditions. Behind it is 1089 (IU-16-58), a Volvo B59 with a Caetano B34D body that dated from March 1976. (PM Photography)

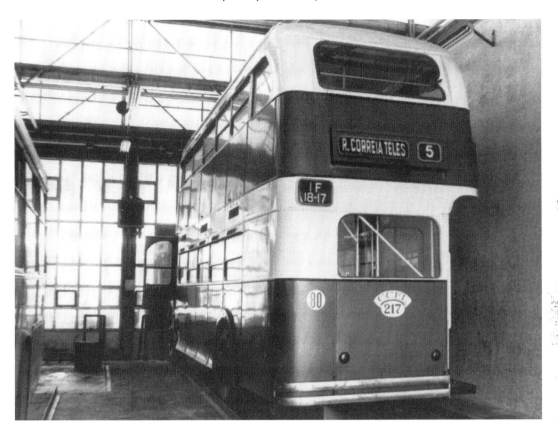

### 233 (HE-18-64)

*Above*: Still painted in its original 1952 livery, Weymann-bodied AEC Regent III 9631E 233 (HE-18-64) is in the Praça do Comércio, in the heart of Lisbon. It is working on the 9 route on 19 July 1964. 'You either love it or hate it' was the slogan for the quintessential British Bovril, but surely not in Lisbon! Sold in a distinctive, bulbous jar, Bovril is a thick and salty beef paste, developed in 1870 by John Lawson Johnston, a Scotsman who sold his mixture to the French during the Franco-Prussian war of 1870–71. It can be made into a beef tea drink by diluting with hot water or as a flavouring for soups, broth, stews and as a meat spread. (A. D. Packer)

### 221 (BD-18-48) and 211 (IG-18-12)

*Opposite above*: Dumped in Santo Amaro Garage yard in the blisteringly hot summer heat of August 1988 are two long unused AEC Regent III 9613Es with Weymann H37/28R bodywork. On the right is 221 (BD-18-48), numbered V14 in the ancillary fleet since December 1983 and although it has obviously not turned a wheel in months it was still officially on the stocks and was not withdrawn until November 1988. On the left is 211 (IG-18-12), which had been taken out of service in January 1982 and slowly stripped of parts, including the nearside mudguard. In the distance between the two is 425 (HH-97-97), an AEC Regent V with a UTIC H40/3F body dating from 1961. From June 1983 it had been painted in an all-over white livery and used as an exhibition bus and a sales stand for vintage tram system tours until 2002. It then served as a snack bar at Aveiro University. (D. R. Harvey)

### 229 (EI-18-62)

*Opposite below*: Loading up in Rossio Square in August 1981 is 229 (EI-18-62), which had entered service in August 1952. This was another Weymann-bodied exposed radiator AEC Regent III 9631E. Rossio is one of Lisbon's many beautiful squares, lined with trees and excellent cafés, bars and restaurants. The square was built well after the earthquake in the Pombaline style with mosaic frontages and shuttered windows and has many later nineteenth-century neoclassical buildings. The centre of the square has two monumental baroque fountains and an 88-foot-high monument with a statue to Dom Pedro IV was erected in 1874. (D. R. Harvey)

**250 (GE-20-85)**

*Above*: Although the guttering still extends over both saloon side windows it is not a deep as on some other buses, having also lost the ventilation slots in the gutters. The ribbing on the curved profile of the roof was designed to dissipate rainwater provided by the heavy spring storms.

**255 (GB-21-07)**

*Opposite above*: After its withdrawal in early 1983, 255 (GB-21-07) was bought by preservationists in England and returned to the country of its birth as the most original of the surviving Weymann H37/28R-bodied AEC Regent III 9613Es. Built and exported in 1954, it entered service on 30 October 1954. Twenty-nine years later it was withdrawn in March 1983 after a long, hard life on the hilly and cobbled streets of Lisbon. The AEC Regal Mark III and Regent III 9631 chassis series were left-hand drive, 8 ft wide and both had a wheelbase of 17 ft 6 in. and overall length of 27 ft 6 in. Purchased by John Shearman direct from Carris, 255 departed Lisbon on 17 April 1983; it was driven through Portugal to Santander and shipped to Plymouth. Now registered KSV 102, it is seen parked at Duxford Museum on the occasion of the Showbus Rally in September 2010. (D. R. Harvey)

**258 (IC-21-63)**

*Opposite below*: Parked in Rossio on 16 July 1964 is 258 (IC-21-63). This AEC Regent 9631E had a Weymann H30/26R body and entered service in February 1955. These twenty-four buses were numbered 249–272 and were among the last Regent IIIs to be built before the model was replaced by the lighter Regent V chassis. Parked behind the bus is a quite unusual Ford 100E Escort estate car, which was derived from the Thames 103E 5 cwt van and trimmed with the same fittings as the two-door Anglia saloon. (A. D. Packer)

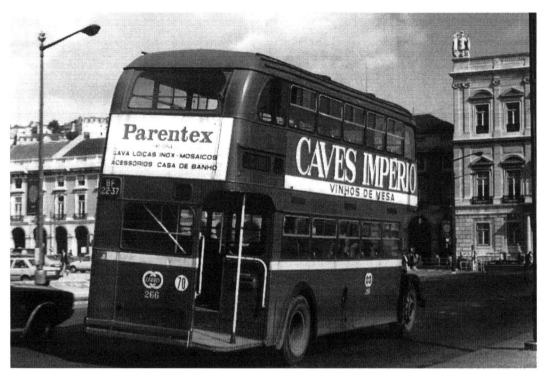

### 266 (BF 22-27)

Passing through the Praça do Comércio is 266 (BF 22-27), an AEC Regent III 9613E in near original condition. Painted in the mid-1960s livery of all-over green with a single cream stripe, the nearside of the Weymann body is a total mirror image of UK-operated open rear platform double-deckers. Afterwards it was rebuilt into a semi-convertible open-top bus for summer tourist trips around the capital in November 1985 and renumbered 21. (PM Photography)

### 266 (BF 22-27)

In August 1988, 266 (BF 22-27) had its Weymann H30/26R bodywork well disguised when it was converted to a semi-convertible open-top bus. At Miraflores Garage the bus was driven out to be posed for a photograph. Rather than have a complete lift-off upper saloon roof, the bus is equipped with a stretched canvas canopy for use in the spring when heavy rainstorms frequently occur. Despite all the hard work during the conversion, it was sold for further use in June 1991. (D. R. Harvey)

**269 (EA-22-20)**

*Above*: With passengers getting off and a queue of waiting customers about to get on, 269 (EA-22-20), which had entered service in June 1955, stands between the grand buildings on the north side of the Praça do Comércio and the 3-ft gauge tram tracks in 1957. This Weymann-bodied AEC Regent III 9613E is still in mint condition with the chromed front bumper still straight and without dents. 269 was finally withdrawn in June 1983. (R. F. Mack)

**272 (LB-22-34)**

*Below*: The last of the 1955 batch of AEC Regent III 9631Es was Weymann H32/26R-bodied 272 (LB-22-34), which entered service in July 1955. It is turning in almost the same radius as the tram lines in the Praça do Chile halfway along Avenida Reis Almirante, between the Baixa and the Avenida João XXI ring road. 272 is working on the 6 route as it negotiates the traffic island in the tree-lined Praça on 18 July 1964. (A. D. Packer)

## 277 (CA-23-63)

*Above*: Being overtaken by a Vauxhall Velox PAD taxi is a Carris double-decker in its original green livery in the early 1960s. Working on the 6 route to Praça Paiva Couceiro is 277 (CA-23-63), an AEC Regent III 9613E with a Weymann H32/26R body new in April 1956. It is passing over some recently abandoned tram tracks in the Avenida da Liberdade and, although well loaded in the lower saloon, is empty upstairs! 277 was withdrawn from service in June 1976. (D. R. Harvey Collection)

## 284 (BL-23-97)

*Below*: Former bus 284 (BL-23-97) joined the ancillary fleet as V2 in July 1979 and survived until July 1988. The Weymann body was painted in an all-over orange livery and had its upper saloon windows painted over, though retaining a full complement of seats in the lower saloon. It was used for staff transport as well as other menial tasks and, like most of these reserve fleet buses, it led an unloved life with a minimum of maintenance. This Weymann-bodied AEC Regent III 9613E is discretely parked in a half-forgotten corner of Santo Amaro Garage yard in August 1981. (D. R. Harvey)

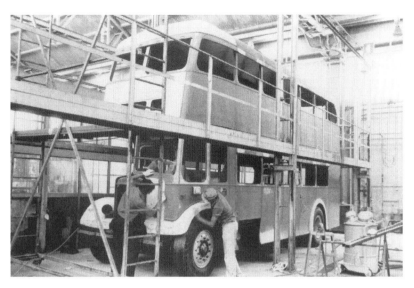

**301 (DD-56-73)**
*Above*: Being brought back to life in the workshops at Miraflores Garage Works as a preserved double-decker in August 1988, this is 301 (DD-56-73). This bus is an AEC Regent V D2LA with a Weymann H32/26R body. Delivered in July 1957, it entered service three months later before being withdrawn in August 1981 and transferred in December 1983 to the ancillary fleet as its V14. The restoration work was very extensive as the bus had been out in the open with only occasional use and suffered the ravages of both the heavy seasonal rainstorms and the summer heat. The cab apron and front wing are being sanded off, but there is still a lot to do with the interior of the body shell devoid of anything, sans seats, wiring and window glass! (D. R. Harvey)

**301 (DD-56-73)**
*Below*: Thirty-one years later, 301 (DD-56-73) is parked outside in the Carris Museum at the rear of Santo Amaro depot yard. On 4 May 2019 301 stands alongside the preserved UTIC-bodied Guy Victory CVU6LX 76 (HL-32-18). The AEC Regent V has a Weymann H32/26R body and entered service in July 1957, and was one of the last Regent Vs to enter service with an exposed radiator. (D. R. Harvey)

## 303 (BD-42-11)

*Above*: About to leave Santo Amaro Garage yard in August 1988 is 303 (BD-42-11), an AEC Regent V D2LA with a Weymann H32/26R body, by now reseated to H37/28R. 303 was one of the 287–314 batch of buses, which were the first Regent Vs in the Lisbon bus fleet. The bus entered service in October 1957 and in terms of appearance looked the same as the earlier Regent IIIs, especially as the exposed radiator versions retained the more substantial Regent III front axle. Although first withdrawn in late 1982, the bus was still in service six years later, albeit somewhat battered and bruised. (D. R. Harvey)

## 308 (BD-42-10) and 270 (EI-22-24)

*Below*: Parked in Praça do Comércio in August 1981 is 308 (BD-42-10), an AEC Regent V D2LA introduced in October 1957. Behind it is 270 (EI-22-24), an AEC Regent III 9631E which is just over two years older. Both buses have Weymann bodies but the one on 308 has had its saloon windows reglazed in rubber. Both have a fluid flywheel, a four-speed pre-selector gearbox and AEC A218 9.6-litre engines. Although both buses have the green and white livery, 279 has the 1970 livery with only a single green stripe. (D. R. Harvey)

## 3. Early Concealed Radiator AEC Regent Vs

### 316 (IF-35-38)

*Above*: The next batch of AEC Regent Vs were numbered between 315 and 370. They differed from the earlier Regent Vs by having the still fairly new design of AEC concealed radiator cowling and were built to the LD2LA specification. This left-hand drive chassis had an 18 ft 7 in. wheelbase and was equipped with an AEC A218 9.6-litre engine coupled to a fluid flywheel and an air-operated four-speed epicyclic gearbox. They were also fitted with front-entrance sixty-seven-seater 30-foot-long Weymann bodywork. 316 (IF-35-38) entered service in November 1958 and is parked in Largo Do Lavra. This is at the bottom of the almost 200-yard-long, 1 in 4 Lavra funicular, which opened on 19 April 1884. This funicular, as well as those at Bica, opened in 1892 and Gloria opened in 1885 and was declared a National Monument in 2003. (G. Morant)

### 326 (IF-39-95)

*Below*: Waiting to start on its next trip to Cais do Sodré, this is 326 (IF-39-95), one of the 315–352 class of Weymann-bodied, 30-foot-long, front-entrance, sixty-seven-seater AEC Regent V LD2LAs. The bus was fitted with an AEC 9.6-litre direct-injection oil engine coupled to an air-operated epicyclic gearbox. 326 is already well filled with passengers as it waits in the tree-lined Rossio Square on 16 July 1964 with all its quarter-drop saloon windows opened. (A. D. Packer)

### 338 (IF-88-74)

*Above*: Withdrawn in Miraflores Garage dump is 338 (IF-88-74), which entered service in November 1959. The AEC Regent V LD2LA had a Weymann H36/31F body and had been in store for over five years. 338 was never repainted in the newer orange and white CCFL livery while 643 (AI-90-22), a CCFL-bodied Regent V, and 672 (HF-27-21), a UTIC-AEC Regent V, both dating from 1964, are also withdrawn but are in the later livery. It was a very hot day in August 1988 which is why your author and a CCFL official are standing in the shade of another withdrawn bus. (D. J. Harvey)

### 349 (IF-77-96)

*Opposite above*: Turning on a pavé road surface at the Xabregas terminus on the 25 route is Weymann-bodied AEC Regent V LD2LA 349 (IF-77-96), which entered service in January 1959. It is Saturday 22 July 1967 and some eighteen months previously this bus had been reseated by six to a H40/33F configuration. Standing in front of a wine warehouse there is a long line of intending passengers who are going into central Lisbon. The bus will terminate in the Praça do Comércio. (A. D. Packer)

**353 (EA-38-58)**
*Below*: Crossing the Avenida da Liberdade is a concealed radiator AEC Regent V LD2LA. This bus had a Weymann H36/31F body which was by now moving away from its British origins. It had deeper equal-height saloon windows with half-drop windows in every bay. 353 (EA-38-58) is in the later green livery with slightly more white. It is working on the 22 route and is being overtaken by a Peugeot 404 saloon with a Pininfarina-styled body resembling the BMC Austin A55 family. (D. R. Harvey Collection)

**364 (BF-50-23)**
*Above*: Travelling along the Avenida da Liberdade is 1960-vintage AEC Regent V LD2LA
364 (BF-50-23). Throughout the first thirty years of bus operation in Lisbon, the vehicles were
always kept in immaculate condition. The green and white livery gave further credence to their
excellent appearance. This CCFL-bodied bus is working on the 23 route and is passing the late
nineteenth-century hotels that line this wide thoroughfare. (PM Photography)

**381 (BL-35-19), 347 (IF-72-55)**
*Below*: Standing double-parked and still picking up and setting down passengers in the Praça do
Comércio are 381 (BL-35-19) and 347 (IF-72-55). 381, on the right, is an AEC Regent V LD2LA
with a CCFL H36/31F body built in April 1961 but reseated to H40/33F some five years later.
It is working on the 46 service and has the original green livery with cream window surrounds.
Parked alongside it is 347 (IF-72-55), another AEC Regent V LD2LA but with a subtly different
Weymann forward-entrance body dating to January 1960. (D. R. Harvey Collection)

**389 (CE-29-55)**

*Above*: Crossing the Avenida da Liberdade when operating on the 5A service is CCFL-bodied AEC Regent V LD2LA 389 (CE-29-55), which had entered service in July 1961. 389 still retains its original green livery with a white roof and saloon windows. It is being overtaken by an East German-built 896cc two-stroke engined DKW Sonderklasse two-door saloon. It is 14 July 1964 and this particular Tuesday must have been a very hot day as not only were all the saloon windows open, but the driver has got his windscreen open. (A. D. Packer)

**413 (BL-42-55)**

*Below*: The original cream and white livery is still being carried by this front-entrance UTIC-bodied AEC Regent V, 413 (BL-42-55). On 19 July 1964, it is parked at Belem, which is located 3½ miles west of the city centre at the mouth of the River Tagus. Many of Lisbon's historic buildings and landmarks are located in Belem, including the fifteenth-century Jerónimos Monastery and the early sixteenth-century Tower of Belém. More recently, erected in 1960, is the Monument to the Discoveries, located on the northern bank of the Tagus. This 170-foot-high concrete slab was built to commemorate the 500th anniversary of the death of Henry the Navigator. (A. D. Packer)

### 418 (BA-26-35)

*Above*: Parked in the shadow of the Ponte 25 de Abril, in the Santo Amaro garage yard, in the summer of 1981 is 418 (BA-26-35). This UTIC-bodied AEC Regent V was in fine fettle and would remain in service for another three years. The forward-entrance UTIC bodies were constructed in Lisbon and could be distinguished from other bodies mounted on Regent Vs by the slightly deeper saloon-side windows. The 25 de Abril Bridge is a suspension bridge connecting the city of Lisbon to the municipality of Almada on the left (south) bank of the Tagus River. It was inaugurated on 6 August 1966 and, until the Carnation Revolution, was named the Salazar Bridge. When it was built it was the fifth largest suspension bridge in the world with a 3,323-foot-long main span and the roadway standing 230 ft above the River Tagus. (D. R. Harvey)

### 426 (HH-97-96)

*Below*: Preserved by the Carris AEC Preservation Group, this is 426 (HH-97-96). This AEC Regent V LD2LA was new in November 1961 and has a UTIC H40/33F body. These large 30-foot-long double-deckers pounded the cobbled, hilly streets of the Portuguese capital for around twenty-five years and it was a testament to the maintenance of the Carris company that they survived for so long. It ran in Lisbon until 1984 before being brought back to the UK for preservation in 1986, whereupon it was registered VVS 337. It is seen attending the Showbus Rally in Duxford and is in the 1960s orange and white livery of Carris. (D. Hill)

**428 (IA-37-16)**

*Above*: With hardly a saloon window opened in the correct position, 428 (IA-37-16), a UTIC H40/33F-bodied AEC Regent V LD2LA of April 1961, stands in the Praça do Comércio. It is still in the all-over green livery in September 1978, but the state of the half-drop windows and some slight rippling of the cantrail side panels below the large BLAUPUNKT advertisement suggest that all is not well with some of the body frames. 428 was withdrawn in November 1984. (PM Photography)

**429 (IA-37-17)**

*Below*: Surrounded by German cars near to Gomes Freira in Estefânia on 17 July 1964 is 429 (IA-37-17), a 1962 AEC Regent V LD2LA with a UTIC H40/33F body. It is working on the 23 bus route and is travelling over the tram tracks of the 6 route near the Hospital Dona Estefânia. Parked under the trees on the left is a Mercedes-Benz 190 being used as a taxi, while overtaking 429 is a 1958 Ford Taunus 17M and a Volkswagen Beetle is behind the double-decker. (A. D. Packer)

**432 (IA-42-08)**
*Above*: About to leave the bus stop in Praça da Figueira is UTIC-bodied AEC Regent V LD2LA 432 (IA-42-08). The bus entered service in October 1962 and had another two years before it was withdrawn. It is working westwards on the 43 route to Caselas, which lies inland of Belém between the A5 motorway and the Monsanto Forest Park. The Praça da Figueira (Square of the Fig Tree) is a large square in the centre of the Lisbon Baixa. It is part of the city that was re-urbanised after the 1755 Lisbon earthquake. It had previously been occupied by the Hospital Real de Todos os Santos, which was extensively damaged and was demolished around 1775. For many years the square was used as an open market square before taking on the role of an ornamental square. (D. R. Harvey)

**439 (CE-97-07)**
*Below*: The last of the 1962 batch of AEC Regent V LD2LAs was 439 (CE-97-07). It is passing around the Marques de Pombal roundabout just north of the Avenida da Liberdade when operating on the 2 route in September 1983. It had a UTIC H36/31F body when new which, in common with all the front-entrance AEC Regent Vs, was converted to a H40/33F seating layout, in this case taking place in 1966. The bus is carrying an advertisement for VARIG; this was the first airline founded in Brazil, in 1927. From 1965 until 1990, it was Brazil's leading airline, but suffered a slow financial decline before closing down in July 2006. (PM Photography)

# 4. Rebodied Regal Double-Deckers

## 447 (EL-13-58)

*Above*: This AEC Regal III 0963 (EL-13-58) entered the CCFL bus fleet in September 1947 as 64 with a Saunders/CCFL single-decker body with a B24D body layout. A new batch of buses numbered 440–494 was created between 1966 and 1968 by rebodying single-deckers from the original 109–146 series with new UTIC H36/29F bodies. The left-hand drive 0963 and 9631E AEC Regal shared the same wheelbase of 17 ft 6 in. and both could be fitted with bodywork with an overall length of 27 ft 6 in., thus enabling the comparatively easy rebodying of the chassis. As the unrebuilt single-deck Regals were becoming redundant, this was a cheap way to add to the double-deck fleet. It is standing in Pombal on 6 August 1966. (R. Symons)

## 454 (BD-14-01)

*Below*: Situated between the beach area of Belém and the foothills of the Monsanto area, the almost village-like Ajuda was reached by the 14 route. Working into Ajuda on 24 July 1967 is 454 (BD-14-01), formerly Saunders-bodied single-decker 71 which was given a UTIC H36/29F body. The 1948-built chassis is an AEC Regal III 0963 which became a double-decker in 1966. The original green and white roof seen from the offside front does soften the somewhat harsh lines of these forty-six rebodied buses, though the typical Weymann-inspired curves of the driver's cab do not harmonise too well with the rather utilitarian windscreen design. (A. D. Packer)

### 462 (FL-14-89)

*Above*: Formerly Saunders-bodied single-decker 84, AEC Regal III 462 (FL-14-89) is working on the 36 service through the Praça do Comércio on its way to Rossio. The new front-entrance bodies built by UTIC on framework supplied by Weymann with a H36/29F seating layout were hardly a triumph of design. The square windscreen and cab apron had a very 'homemade' appearance while the rear end had a bobtailed look not helped by the near-vertical rear profile. The result was a rather gaunt style of body. The rebodying as double-deckers was necessitated by the need to increase the available number of passenger seats on the intensive Lisbon bus routes. Many of the Saunders bodies on the 1948 AEC Regal III 0963s were coming to the end of their economic lives and their chassis, identical to the contemporary export version of the Regent IIIs, became the obvious choice for this conversion, which took place during 1966. (PM Photography)

### 470 (FA-15-03)

*Below*: 470 (FA-15-03), wearing the drab 1970 near all-over green livery, stands on the forecourt of Santo Amaro Garage in company with similar bus 484 (FL-14-87). 470 was formerly single-deck bus 92 with a Saunders B24D body that was new in October 1948. It was rebodied with the somewhat gaunt-looking UTIC H36/29F in May 1966 and was taken out of service in August 1979, whereas 484, to the right, retained the green and white livery and lasted until February 1980. (D. R. Harvey Collection)

**475 (GD-15-01)**

*Above*: Originally built as Saunders B24D-bodied single-decker 98, an AEC Regal 9631E, 475 (GD-15-01) became a UTIC-bodied forward-entrance double-decker in January 1967, using frames supplied by Weymann, and gave the vehicle another twelve years' service. Parked in the bus station in Cais do Sodré, near to the railway station terminus of the Estoril Railway, the bus still has the original pre-1970 green and white livery. (D. R. Harvey Collection)

**491 (ID-15-08)**

*Below*: 491 (ID-15-08), formerly Saunders-bodied single-decker 24, was one of the last five AEC Regal III 0963s to be rebodied as a double-decker. Unlike the other buses the contract was undertaken by CCFL and occurred in the spring of 1968, some eighteen months after the last of the UTIC-rebodies. Remaining in service until June 1983, the bus has acquired possibly one of the most narrow and therefore unreadable destination boxes imaginable! 491 is parked in the Praça do Comércio towards the end of its operational career. (PM Photography)

## 5. The Last Half-Cab Double-Deckers

### 615 (CE-97-11)

*Above*: About to leave for Marvila, this is AEC Regent LD2LA 615 (CE-97-11), with a sixty-seven seat CCFL-body. It is in the Praça do Comércio in September 1978 and is in the near all-over green 1970 livery. This 30-foot-long bus, in this livery, could almost fit into the landscape of any provincial town in the UK, save of course that the cab and entrance are the wrong way round. Even the offside rear emergency door looks almost like a set of small platform doors. The interdeck panels on 615 have a large advertisement for Tudor batteries, a French multi-national supplier of mainly batteries for road vehicles who in later years would be taken over by the Exide company. (PM Photography)

### 603 (CE-91-57)

*Opposite above*: Parked near to the beach at Estoril in July 1988 is 603 (CE-91-57), being used as a snack bar. Somehow the CCFL bodywork on this AEC Regent V LD2LA, now painted white, looks less fussy than when it was being operated by Carris in Lisbon. Although 603 looks complete, it was sold without its AEC A222 engine and had been recently towed to this location, having been withdrawn in 1985. At this time buses like this were being sold off as engineless vehicles for subsequent use as cafés, bars, shops and even store sheds. (D. R. Harvey)

### 604 (CE-91-58)

*Opposite below*: Standing at the bus stop in Rossio is 604 (CE-91-58), which has been repainted into the predominantly green livery. This bus was the fifth in the 600–644 group of AEC Regent Vs with CCFL H36/31F bodies and was delivered in March 1962. Like all the front-entrance Regent Vs delivered with this sixty-seven-seater layout, its capacity was increased to H40/33F; in this case, the extra six seats were added to the bus in May 1968. 604 lasted in service until November 1984 before it was taken out of service. (PM Photography)

### 622 (IA-57-53)

*Above*: On a damp-looking day in Rossio Square, 622 (IA-57-53) stands at a bus stop while working on the 39 route. It is the winter of 1974 in Rossio, with leafless trees lining the square in front of the many nearly empty cafés and bars while 622 loads up potential passengers. This AEC Regent V LD2LA has a CCFL H40/33F body and is by now painted in the Carris livery of orange and white. The bus entered service in June 1962 and was not withdrawn until 1988. (D. Withers)

### 626 (EL-31-24)

*Opposite above*: Travelling eastwards on Avenida Infante Dom Henrique alongside the River Tagus to the left and across the Praça do Comércio is 626 (EL-31-24), working on the 39 route. The AEC Regent V LD2LA has a CCFL H40/33F body and dates from October 1963. It is late in the career of this bus as behind is an unidentified Iveco 470 with a brand new Salvador Caetano B41D body built in 1983, thus dating this scene to about 1983, the year before 626 was withdrawn. (PM Photography)

### 633 (IA-76-91)

*Opposite below*: The long 29 route travelled along the north bank of the River Tagus via Ajuda before reaching its terminus at Belem. 633 (IA-76-91), another 30-foot-long forward-entrance AEC Regent V, is speeding towards Belem on 24 July 1967. The bus is barely five years old and looks in pristine condition in its equally divided green and white livery. The only part of the CCFL body design that lacks 'inspiration' is at the back of the bus, where the rather squared-off rear dome and back saloon windows are not really in keeping with the more curvaceous frontal appearance. (A. D. Packer)

## 648 (II-43-68)
*Above*: Travelling over the cobbles alongside warehouses at the side of the River Tagus is 648 (II-43-68). This was one of the fifty-seven 645–701 class of UTIC-AEC U2007s whose chassis were assembled from imported Regent V parts. Although they had UTIC-AEC chassis plates, they also retained their LD2LA numbers. These buses were equipped with the AEC A222 11.3-litre left-handed engine, which enabled these buses to storm up the steep hills in the Bairro Alto, Graça and Alfama areas of Lisbon with impunity. The bus is travelling towards the city terminus at São Bento, opposite the Portuguese parliament buildings, from Marvila, which would become the last route to be worked by the crew-operated Regent Vs. (D. R. Harvey)

## 662 (CB-45-51)
*Below*: The suburb of Lumiar is in the north of Lisbon, to the west of Lisbon Airport. 1964-vintage UTIC-AEC Regent U2007 662 (CB-45-51) was one of the 645–701 class assembled by UTIC from bought-in chassis parts. It is seen parked alongside the railway station in Estrada da Todre on 22 July 1967. The design of these 30-foot-long double-deckers was clearly derived from the original imported rear-entrance Regent IIIs of 1950, particularly in the arrangement around the cab door and the curved tumblehome on the lower panels. (A. D. Packer)

## 678 (FE-32-75)

*Above*: Travelling towards Praça Marqués de Pombal in Avenida da Liberdade is 678 (FE-32-75). This 30-foot-long double-decker was a UTIC-AEC U2007 with a UTIC H40/33F body dating from March 1965. The colour co-ordinated advertisement for the bathroom fitment manufacturer Valadares matches the orangey-yellow and white livery of the bus. Avenida da Liberdade is a 100-yard-wide, 1,200-yard-long boulevard, with ten lanes divided by pedestrian pavements decorated with gardens. Linking Restauradores Square with Marquis of Pombal Square, the avenue was built between 1879 and 1886 and was modelled on the boulevards of Paris. (D. R. Harvey)

## 679 (FE-32-63)

*Below*: On the Rua do Grilo, coming into the Beato area to the north-east of the city centre, is 679 (FE-32-63), belching out a quite considerable amount of exhaust smoke as it accelerates downhill. It is working in from the Marvila terminus on the 39 route on 21 August 1986 over the cobbled road surface and the tram tracks of the 16 and 27 services to Xabregas and Poco do Bispo. This UTIC-AEC U2007 with a UTIC H40/33F body dating from March 1965 had only about sixteen more months on service before its withdrawal from public service. (P. J. Thompson)

### 684 (CE-31-58)
*Above*: The driver of 684 (CE-31-58), a UTIC-bodied UTIC-AEC U2007, waits for the intending passengers to get onto his charge when working on the 2 route to the railway station at Campolide to the north-west of central Lisbon. It is parked in the Praça Dom Pedro IV, locally known as Rossio Square, during the very hot August of 1981, alongside the pavements lined with trees that afford a little protection from the heat. The shops and bars all have their colourful canvas blinds pulled down in order to offer some more shade. (D. R. Harvey)

### 693 (FE-73-33)
*Below*: Leaving behind the imposing Avenida Palace Hotel, built in 1892, in the distant Rua 1st Dezembro, 693 (FE-73-33), a UTIC-bodied Regent IV, has crossed the small Praça Dom Joao Câmara and is about to turn into Rossio Square when working on the 39 service. This UTIC front-entrance bus was built in 1965 and would stay operational until September 1991. Surrounded by heavy traffic travelling into the north-west corner of Rossio, the bus is being overtaken by a typical black-and-grey-painted Mercedes-Benz 250 taxi. (D. R. Harvey Collection)

### 700 (LE-53-14) and 824 (LB-76-27)

*Above*: Standing next to marketplace awnings in the bus station at Cais do Sodré in August 1981 are two British imports of a very different hue. On the left is 700 (LE-53-14), a UTIC H40/33F-bodied UTIC-AEC U2007 built in August 1965 and the penultimate one of the batch of locally assembled double-deckers representing the typical Lisbon half-cab bus. Alongside it is the rear-engined 824 (LB-76-27). This 1967-built bus was a Daimler Fleetline CRG6LXB and had a CCFL H45/34F body. In later years it would be converted to an open-top tourist bus with a much reduced seating capacity of only fifty-eight. (D. R. Harvey)

### 704 (GB-82-54) and 726 (DB-72-73)

*Below*: At the Praça São Bento terminus on 17 August 1987 are two of the 1967 batch of AEC Regent V LD2LAs. The702–731 class represented the last British-built half-cab double-deckers delivered to Lisbon. 704 (GB-82-54) and 726 (DB-72-73) entered service in April 1966 and January 1967 respectively and were bodied by Carris itself, though the usual H40/33F seating layout was retained. The between-decks advertisement for TABOPAN, a natural wood furniture veneer, on 704 compares somewhat unfavourably with the unadorned yellow and white livery of 726, but such were the needs to obtain more revenue! (P. J. Thompson)

### 705 (GB-97-70)
*Above*: Hard at work on the 39 route is 705 (GB-97-70). This AEC Regent V LD2LA has a Carris-built H40/33F body and entered service in 1967. On 21 August 1986 the bus is travelling along Trevessa da Manutençao in the Xabregas area of eastern Lisbon, over the tram tracks formerly used by the 16 route between Belem, Praça do Comércio and Xabregas. Following the Regent is 2113 (NS-71-46), a MAN SL200F with a Caetano B41D body dating from October 1985 and typical of the type of single-decker bought by CCFL throughout the 1980s. (P. J. Thompson)

### 706 (FG-41-99)
*Below*: This is why the big AEC A222 11.3-litre engine was needed! The need for a large and powerful engine on Lisbon's steep hills on either side of the Baixa is well shown as 706 (FG-41-99), a CCFL-bodied AEC Regent V LD2LA, negotiates the sharp turn into Calçada do Grilo from Calçada de Dom Gastao when working on the 3 route on Thursday 21 August 1986. The bus has a large advertisement for TRIUNFO biscuits and wafers. (P. J. Thompson)

### 708 (GI-62-25)

*Above*: About to enter the Praça do Comércio from the deep shadows of the Rua Aurea, one of the main shopping streets in the Baixa, in August 1985 is 708 (GI-62-25). Entering service in June 1966, with a body entirely constructed by CCFL, these buses in the 702–731 series were nominally AEC Regent Vs but with the UTIC U2007 chassis type, despite having a normal LD2LA chassis number. Fitted with the usual Monocontrol transmission, this was virtually the only concession to make the driver's life easier. Noteworthy is the appalling state of the road surface next to the tram tracks, which has been broken up by the constant pounding by the trams and ordinary vehicular traffic. (D. R. Harvey)

### 721 (FC-81-57)

*Below*: Standing in Rossio during August 1981 in the green livery with a single white band is AEC Regent V LD2LA721 (FC-81-57). By now nearly fifteen years old, it would continue in service for another five years. Carrying an advertisement for shaving foam, the bus appears to be getting near to its seventy-three-seat capacity. Behind the AEC is a French Citröen DS saloon and a Volvo B59 single-decker with a Caetano body dating from about 1976. (D. R. Harvey)

**723 (GL-46-31)**
Having left the main shopping area in Lisbon's city centre, CCFL H40/33F-bodied AEC Regent V
LD2LA 723 (GL-46-31) passes around the Marques de Pombal roundabout at the top end of
the Avenida da Liberdade and is facing the ornamental Eduardo VII Park. The well-loaded bus is
in the yellow/orange and white livery and carries an advertisement for MABOR tyres. 723 had
entered service in November 1966 and was withdrawn in January 1991. (D. R. Harvey Collection)

# 6. Underfloor-Engined 1960s Single-Deckers

**63 (DB-72-71)**
Travelling along the Rua da Conceiçao behind the impressive buildings in the Praça do Comércio
in August 1988 is 63 (DB-72-71). This AEC Reliance 2U2LA with a four-speed Monocontrol
gearbox was one of six numbered 61–66 that entered service in January 1967. It is working over
the 3-ft gauge tram tracks on the 67 service to the castle. Seating only eighteen passengers with
fifty-two standees and three doors when new, they soon became unpopular with the travelling
public and were rebuilt with a B26 + 34T layout in 1984. (D. R. Harvey)

**65 (DB72-70)**

*Above*: Loading up with passengers in Rossio is AEC Reliance U2013 2U2LA 65 (DB72-70). These buses, bodied by UTIC despite their length, only had a B18T layout but had room for large numbers of standees. This 'cramming them in' approach proved unpopular and all the class were rebuilt with a B26T layout in 1984, surviving in this form until January 1992. The bus later became part of the auxiliary fleet as number V4. (PM Photography)

**66 (DB-72-72)**

*Below*: 66 (DB-72-72), a 1967 AEC Reliance U2013 2U2LA, passes the Escola Boys Primary School No. 3 in the Rua António Sérgio in the Baixa in August 1988. The reseated UTIC B26T bodywork looks in need of some extensive remedial work judging by the state of the crooked half-drop windows and the panelling, but despite its condition, the AEC 9.6-litre AH 590 engine was removed and the six buses were re-engined with a Volvo HD100A engine, also of 9.6-litre capacity, in 1989. 66 was not withdrawn until March 1993. (D. R. Harvey)

### 68 (LB-59-38)

*Above*: The Praça do Comércio was served by both trams and buses with a lot of the traffic travelling on an east to west axis parallel to the River Tagus waterfront. In August 1988, on the left, is equal-wheel bogie tram 351. It has just terminated its journey on the 15 route from Estádio, Alges and Belem. This 17½-ton forty-seat tram was built by J. Stephenson in New York in 1906 and rebuilt in about 1960. The unidentified four-wheeler has travelled into the city on the 18 tram route from Ajuda and Alcântara, passing near to the Santo Amaro tram depot en route. The three-doored single-decker bus is 68 (LB-59-38), the second of the twenty buses that were sold to Lisbon as Daimler Freelines at the same time that CCFL was purchasing its Daimler Fleetline double-deckers. In reality the chassis were actually Guy Victory CVU6LXs. 68 had a UTIC B18D body and entered service in August 1967. For the same reason as the AEC Reliances, it was reconfigured to a B26T layout in 1984, running until 1991 before becoming numbered V6 in the ancillary fleet. (D. R. Harvey)

### 75 (HL-32-19)

*Below*: Parked near to Cais do Sodré when working on the 15 service is Guy Victory CVU6LX 75 (HL-32-19) with a UTIC B26T body, although CCFL referred to the twenty buses as Daimler Freelines. It entered service in September 1967 and still has its original green livery with a single white-painted waistrail band. 75 is being operated with a conductor though they were latterly operated as OMO vehicles. (PM Photography)

**82 (HL-50-36)**

Not so much parked but abandoned at Cais do Sodré in August 1981 is UTIC-bodied Guy Victory CVU6LX 82 (HL-50-36). It is being used as an OMO vehicle and carries the AUTOMATIZADA plate next to the front entrance. With the River Tagus and the landing stage in the distance, the bus has gone around the Mercado de Lisboa, with its numerous fish and fruit and vegetable stalls, before heading back to Sete Rios on the 15 route. This bus service acted as a link between the latter's mainline Lisbon railway station in the north of the city and the adjacent Cais do Sodré railway station for services to Estoril. 82 was the first of the class to be withdrawn, having been destroyed by a fire in November 1989. (D. R. Harvey)

# 7. Rear-Engined Daimler Fleetlines

**801 (GL-52-30)**

Turning into the Praça do Comércio from Rua Aurea in August 1985 is 801 (GL-52-30). This was the first of the fifty Daimler Fleetline CRG6LXBs with CCFL H45/34F bodywork and was the only one to be delivered in 1966. The bodywork on these buses had distinct echoes of early 1960s Metro-Cammell designs, but heavily disguised by deep half-drop windows, a sun visor above the windscreen and the rows of guttering on the roof cantrail. The bus is carrying an advertisement for VARIG, which at the time was the oldest and largest Brazilian airline, but which went bankrupt in July 2006. 801 was eventually withdrawn in February 1991. (D. R. Harvey)

**806 (LG-66-08)**

*Above*: Leaving a bus stop in the tree-lined Avenida da Liberdade when working on the 39 route is CCFL-bodied Daimler Fleetline CRG6LXB 806 (LG-66-08). July 1988 was part of a very hot summer but it is perhaps surprising that the only opened windows on the double-decker are the front ones in the upper saloon. This attractive-looking seventy-nine-seater entered service in April 1967 and was taken out of service in August 1995. (D. R. Harvey)

**818 (ID-67-08)**

*Below*: Working on the Linha Verde *(where have I heard that before?)* at Lisbon Airport is 818 (ID-67-08). It is in the 'trendy' green and white livery of the buses designated for the Green Line service which really doesn't quite suit the body style of these CCFL-bodied Daimler Fleetline buses. 818 is about to return to the city centre of Lisbon on the 90 limited stop express service, though with the thin aperture of the destination box it is a little difficult to tell where it is going! (D. R. Harvey)

**824 (LB-76-27)**
*Above*: With the open-air market in Cais de Sodré in the background, Daimler Fleetline CRG6LXB 824 (LB-76-27) is parked between the bus shelters in the row that includes the stop for the 44 route. This stop is within a few minutes' walk of the interurban railway to Estoril. The bus is working on the 44 route and has nearly all its half-drop windows in the open position. As with all the Daimler Fleetlines, the bus has retained its decorative front wheel nut guard rings. (D. R. Harvey)

**830 (HL-88-57)**
*Below*: Loading up with passengers on a wet day in Rossio is 830 (HL-88-57). The CCFL body had a H45/34F seating layout and despite having a rear engine the big Gardner 10.45-litre engine seemed surprisingly adept at coping with the high summer temperatures. These buses carried the fluted Daimler badge placed prominently on the front apron. These buses had a surprisingly long life, many lasting until the early 1990s, being used latterly on the airport service while a few were converted to open-top condition for some of the earliest Lisbon City tours. 830 is being used on the 39 route with a 1980 Camo B38D-bodied Volvo B10R, 1409 (BV-92-22), behind it. (A. Greaves)

### 852 (CG-60-98)

*Above*: Passing through Rossio Square, with its wavy patterned mosaic pavement, is the first of the four Daimler Fleetline CRG6LXBs with rather square-looking Caetano H47/25D bodywork that were delivered in March 1972. 852 was painted in a very unusual, eye-catching livery that made it look like two single-decker buses were on top of each other. These buses represented the final flourish of new British-built double-deckers in Lisbon, with this bus being withdrawn in September 1992. (D. R. Harvey)

### 835 (BG-44-51)

*Opposite above*: Freshly repainted Daimler Fleetline CRG6LXB 835 (BG-44-51) is about to pull away while working on the 219 service when parked at a bus stop in Rua Quirino da Fonsera, near to the Praça de Chile, on 18 August 1987. The attractive CCFL H47/34F bodywork has strong echoes of British coachbuilders' designs though the frontal appearance is rather spoilt by the tiny single-aperture front destination box. (P. J. Thompson)

### 845 (IB-86-85)

*Opposite below*: Pulling into a bus stop in Dom Luís V Square in August 1988 is 845 (IB-86-85). This Daimler Fleetline CRG6LX was new in December 1968 and has a rather attractive British-looking CCFL-built H45/34F body. Notable is that these batch of Fleetlines had the latest style of rear engine bonnet assembly with a large removable panel to gain access to the Gardner 10.45-litre engine. The bus has reverted to destination boxes of a suitable depth (i.e. they can be read!), and so the bus can be identified as working on the 29 service to São Bento. (D. R. Harvey)

**925 (TA-46-45)**
*Above*: About to leave the bus stop at Cais do Sodré is the last double-decker to be operated from new in Lisbon. Numbered 925 (TN-46-43), this was a Leyland Olympian ONTL11/2L demonstrator with an ECW H47/31D body which entered service in the capital in July 1982 suitably adorned with the words 'Leyland Olympian'. It had left Lisbon after a fairly short period of being demonstrated to CCFL, as it next appeared for an exhibition in Brazil. The bus had the same chassis and a similar body style, also built by ECW, to those buses supplied to Athens in March 1983, though these had a H47/26D seating layout. It is probable that 925 was actually intended to go to Greece but was diverted to be tried out in Lisbon. This final attempt by a British bus manufacturer to break back into the Portuguese market was even less successful than the attempt in Greece; Athens at least bought eleven of the model. (D. R. Harvey Collection)

**854 (FH-33-14)**
*Opposite above*: The squared design of the Caetano bodywork built on the final four Daimler Fleetline CRG6LXs supplied to Carris had a resemblance to the contemporary British designs built for London Transport by MCW and Park Royal on the DMS class as well as on bodies being constructed for the newly formed PTEs around England. Noticeable is the centre exit door, which was a feature only found on these four Lisbon double-deck Daimler Fleetlines. 854 (FH-33-14) is at the Marques de Pombal roundabout just north of the Avenida da Liberdade. (PM Photography)

**855 (FH-70-16)**
*Opposite below*: The four Caetano-bodied Daimler Fleetline CRG6LXs were the last new double-deckers purchased by Carris and arrived in March 1972. A further order for twenty-five chassis with numbers 63584–63608 was placed by CCFL but these were cancelled. The rather plain aspect of these Lisbon buses contrasted with the same body-builder's products produced on Leyland Atlantean LPDR1/1s six years earlier between 1966 and 1967 for Oporto. 855 (FH-70-16) is standing in Rossio Square wearing the mainly green livery of the early 1970s. On its offside panels it displays an advertisement for Sagres, one of the most popular Portuguese beers. (PM Photography)

# B. Oporto

Oporto, or Porto, is one of the oldest European cities, dating back to around 300 BC, with Celtic people being the first known inhabitants. Occupied by the Romans, the city developed as an important commercial port. In the fourteenth and fifteenth centuries, Oporto's shipyards contributed to the development of Portuguese shipbuilding. It was also from the port of Oporto that, in 1415, Prince Henry the Navigator (son of King John I of Portugal) embarked on the conquest of the Moorish port of Ceuta, in northern Morocco. This expedition by the king and his fleet was followed by navigation and exploration along the western coast of Africa, initiating the Portuguese Age of Discovery.

During the eighteenth and nineteenth centuries the city became an important industrial centre and saw its size and population increase. Oporto is Portugal's second city; it is a real 'working' city with a large port and shipbuilding facilities and at Matosinhos near to the mouth of the Douro there is a thriving cod and sardine fishing industry. Oporto's historical core was proclaimed a World Heritage site by UNESCO in 1996.

The steeply incised River Douro separates Oporto from Vila Nova da Gaia, famous for its port caves such as Sandeman, Grahams, Dow, Taylors, Warre and Calem, and the two are linked by numerous bridges over the Douro. It cannot be stressed enough how important these bridges are to the economy of Oporto. The Ponte D. Maria is a wrought iron arched railway bridge, designed by Gustave Eiffel and built in 1877. It still stands as a testament to the genius of Eiffel but was made redundant and was closed to rail traffic in 1991. Just downstream is the Dom Luís I Bridge, a double-decked metal arch bridge. It was begun in 1881 and opened on 31 October 1886 and with a span of 564 feet was the longest of its type in the world, with a maximum height of 148 feet. It was designed by a German engineer, Théophile Seyrig, a business partner of Gustave Eiffel. It is significant to the history of transport in Oporto, as for many years trams, trolleybuses and buses used both levels in order to cross the River Douro.

During the twentieth century, further major bridges were built. The Arrábida Bridge, which at its opening had the biggest concrete supporting arch in the world, connects the north and south shores of the Douro on the west side of Oporto. The São João railway bridge, which is 1,247 yards long, was built in 1991 and replaced Eiffel's wrought iron Maria Pia Bridge. The newest bridge is the Ponte do Infante, opened on 24 June 2003. It is a road bridge connecting Vila Nova de Gaia to Oporto and was built to replace the upper board of the Luis I Bridge. The Ponte do Infante bridge is 406 yards long and 22 yards wide, with two lanes in each direction.

The development of public transport in Oporto began when the municipal authorities wished to encourage mule-hauled trams and felt that they should be instrumental in the construction of the tramway along the Marginal (the northern river bank of the River Douro) as they had been responsible for the construction of the highway there from 1854 onwards. The service commenced on 9 March 1872 between Miragaia and Figuera da Foz on a temporary basis with two tramcars, with the official launch taking place on 15 May 1872. Although this was not the first tramway in Portugal, it was the first urban passenger tramway to operate in the country. Disputes between the municipality and the earliest operators were always acrimonious and it was left to a new company, Companhia Carris de Ferro do Porto (CCFP), to expand the network into the city and to other suburban areas.

Mule-hauled trams were replaced with the advent of electrification, beginning in 1895 with a route between Carmo in the city centre and the ports at Leixoes and Matosinhos. In 1906 CCFP constructed an extensive new electric tramway network to serve the city and the surrounding area, including two long routes to Ponte de Pedra and to Ermesinde as well as two services across the upper roadway of the 60-metre-high Dom Luís bridge into Vila Nova de Gaia, south of the Douro. In 1912–13 a new electric tramway, replacing a steam tramway, was built along the extended Avenida dc Boavista to the coast at Castelo do Queijo.

The original fleet of trams had reached the end of their working lives and were in need of urgent modernisation, so that between 1905 and 1912 new tramcars were imported, mostly from the J. G. Brill Co. of Philadelphia, USA, whose semi-convertible deep-window-bodied designs were ideally suited to Portugal's climate. In the mid-1920s CCPT enlarged the workshops at Boavista and began to build complete four-wheel trams, using American trucks and equipment. For many years the Oporto Tramways Company Works built Brill-style semi-convertible four-wheel tramcars.

The first bogie eight-wheel tram was introduced in 1904 and remained unique in the fleet until a total twelve Fumista-type bogie car trams were built before 1930, looking like extended versions of the traditional four-wheel tramcars. In 1929, ten further bogie cars, numbered 280–289, were delivered to Oporto from Belgium; these were very different, having a much more north European appearance. After the war only two dozen more four-wheelers were constructed, while the swan-song was an experimental single-ended tram numbered 500 which was built in 1952. By 1950, CCFP was operating 191 trams and 25 trailers over 51 miles of tram routes. Again, as in Lisbon, the trams were due to be phased out in the 1990s, but a reprieve came in the form of a fleet of restored tramcars and these remain in use.

Throughout the 1930s, the criticism of the slow speed of tram travel continued and the newly formed operator, STCP, eventually placed an order for buses following a tender for fifteen Daimler CVD6s with Auto Triunfo FB34D bodies for delivery in July 1947. The four new bus routes were progressively inaugurated in 1948; these were the C to Carvalhido (from 1 April), the D to Antas (from 1 June), the A to Foz (from 24 June) and the E to Paranhos (from 23 October). A bus garage was built at Carcereira and in 1948 fifteen more Daimler CVD6s with Dalfa FB34D bodies were ordered for delivery in 1949. These were numbered 1–30 and were followed by a batch of eight AEC Regal IIIs (31–38) with full-fronted bodywork built by STCP (Oporto) in the summer of 1952.

Between 1954 and 1957 batches of Daimler Freeline D650HS under-floor single-deckers, numbered 39–51, were delivered with bodies by either Dalfa (46–51) or Estrela (39–45) with a B33D layout. In 1959, an order for ten Leyland Worldmaster LERT1/1s with Dalfa B36D bodywork was placed and these were belatedly followed by

462–506 during the spring and summer of 1967, but this time with Salvador Caetano B38D bodywork. These were the last British-built single-deck chassis to be purchased by Oporto. During this period ten AEC Regent V D2LA double-deckers with UTIC H36/31F bodies (201–210) were acquired in July 1960 to operate a City–Leca de Palmeira service as dock construction and a new bridge at Leixoes required buses for construction workers.

In 1960 the bus livery became turquoise and ivory instead of the brown and cream of the trams and it was soon afterwards that a Leyland Atlantean LPDR1/1 with a Metro-Cammell H36/31F body entered service in May 1962 as fleet number 72 (later 211). This body acted as a prototype for a further nine Atlanteans with MCCW-style bodies built by Salvador Caetano, but with a H41/32F layout. A further batch, numbered 82–111 (later 221–250), had similar-looking bodies by Dalfa and arrived between October 1963 and January 1965 but still looked similar to the original MCCW prototype, which incidentally was immortalised by Dinky Toys. These Dalfa bodies were very similar in appearance to the bodies on the double-deck Lancia trolleybuses numbered 101–150, though these had a two-door layout.

The final order for British-built double-decker buses was for ninety Leyland Atlantean LPDR1/1s numbered 251–340, whose delivery began in September 1966, and it took fourteen months to get all the vehicles into service. They had angular H49/38F Salvador Caetano bodywork with very deep saloon windows and had an attractive grille on the lower front panel for the forward-mounted radiator.

For the next six years, with a struggling economy and political uncertainty rife throughout Portugal, no further new buses were purchased by Oporto. Nevertheless a public tender was placed for 200 buses to be fitted with Portuguese bodies in 1974 and these orders were for 284 Volvo B59s fitted with Salvador Caetano, CAMO and UTIC single-deck bodywork. This spelt the end of British bus purchases in the city just as the same policy was being undertaken in the capital. In 1978/1979 100 MAN SL200s with bodywork split equally between Salvador Caetano and UTIC were ordered.

# 1. The Front-Engined Single-Deckers

**1 (BL-13-41)**

*Above*: The first single-deck motor buses for Oporto were a pair of Daimler CVD6s with full-fronted thirty-four-seat bodywork built by Auto Triunfo bodywork and were new in July 1947. Many of the single-deck buses built for export by Daimler at this time were fitted with the Daimler CD6 8.6-litre engine. Daimlers were all fitted with a fluid flywheel coupled to a Wilson Preselector gearbox producing an extremely smooth-riding bus. 1 (BL-13-41) was rebodied by STCP in its own workshops in 1966 with a FB27D body which gave the bus another ten years of service. It is travelling into the city with its two-door second body in about 1970. (D. R. Harvey Collection)

**2 (DA-13-42)**

*Below*: In July 1947 Oporto initially ordered fifteen Daimler CVD6 chassis, numbered 1–15, of which nine were bodied locally by Auto Triunfo with the balance of the body order going to Dalfa. This was followed by an order for fifteen more in 1948, all of which had Dalfa FB34D bodywork. 2 (DA-13-42) was numerically the first of the thirty Daimler CVD6 chassis with a 19-ft wheelbase to be delivered in July 1947. It is virtually brand new and sports its first single-deck body; it would be rebodied with a replacement Dalfa FB27D body with a concealed radiator during 1967. (D. R. Harvey Collection)

**8 (IF-13-98) and 2 (DA-13-42)**
*Above*: In the Avenida dos Aliados, this Daimler CVD6, IF-13-98, numbered 8 in the Oporto fleet, overtakes the parked 2 (DA-13-42), both of which have Auto Triunfo FB34D bodies. Most of these 1947 chassis were rebodied in 1966, with 2 receiving a Dalfa FB27D body and being renumbered 402. Bus 8 was not so lucky, being one of the eight buses in the class of thirty not to be rebodied by STCP and thus being withdrawn early in April 1970. (D. R. Harvey Collection)

**17 (CE-14-65)**
*Below*: As far as the chassis numbers of the thirty Daimler CVD6s with fleet numbers 1–30 were concerned, the first two had chassis numbered 13591–2, delivered in July 1947, while 3–17 had non-sequential numbers in the 15028–42 chassis number range and came between December 1947 and September 1949. This left 18–30 with chassis numbers 17015–29, which all arrived in February 1949. 17 (CE-14-65), with its replacement 1967-built Dalfa FB27D+22 standee bodywork, crosses the lower deck of the magnificent Dom Luís I Bridge when working on the service to Madalena. This is a suburb of Vila Nova da Gaia and has access to an expanse of magnificent sandy beaches. (R. Symons)

## 22 (IE-15-79)

*Above*: Standing in the Carcereira Garage yard in 26 July 1967 is 22 (IE-15-79), a Daimler CVD6 dating from February 1949. The original Dalfa FB34D body had been partly rebuilt with new glazing but would not be renumbered and was withdrawn by 1975, some three to four years before those Daimlers rebodied in 1967. Carcereira Garage housed both motorbuses, on the right beyond the diesel fuel pumps, and the trolleybus fleet. Just visible to the distant left are some of Oporto's splendid Dalfa-bodied Lancia double-decker trolleybuses. (A. D. Packer)

## 32 (PS-13-57)

*Below*: Parked alongside the River Douro in Vila Nova da Gaia is STCP 32 (PS-13-57), an AEC Regal III 9631E with an STCP FB26D body. Behind the bus, straddling the River Douro, is the double-deck Dom Luís I bridge linking Vila Nova da Gaia to the city of Oporto on the distant bank. In front of the bus are rows of the oak barrels used in the fermentation of port wine. The eight members of this class of Regal IIIs entered service in the summer of 1952 and were numbered 31–38. All were withdrawn without being rebodied in June 1980. (D. R. Harvey Collection)

**35 (PS-13-56)**

An STCP inspector, having spoken to the bus driver, walks around the bus when working on the route to Santo Ovidio, an inner suburb of Vila Nova da Gaia across the River Douro. The multi-windows of the full-fronted STCP B26D bodies were shorter than the bodies on the Daimlers as they had a wheelbase of only 17 ft 6 in. 35 (PS-13-56) has the exposed radiator of the AEC Regal III 9631E chassis incorporated into the full front of the bodywork. (D. R. Harvey Collection)

## 2. Uncertain Ordering Policies in the Early 1960s

**40 (EF-21-42)**

The second of the seven Estrela B33D-bodied Daimler Freeline D650HSs was 40 (EF-21-42). It entered service in March 1955 and is parked in Avenida dos Aliasos in 1974, three years before it was withdrawn. It was later renumbered 440. The Freeline model was Daimler's attempt to break into the underfloor-engined single-deck market to compete with the AEC Regal IV and Leyland Royal Tiger models. It had only reached the production stage in 1952, but Freelines proved to be poor sellers because although a quality product, it was too heavy and thirsty for the home market. As a result most examples were built for export, with the Portuguese bus industry being quite a productive marketplace. (A. R. Phillips)

## 42 (IG-21-69)

*Above*: 42 (IG-21-69) was a Daimler Freeline D650HS with an Estrela B33D multi-windowed body that had cantrail-level standee windows. This was one of the seven Freeline single-deckers numbered 39–45 and was new in March 1955. The D650HS model had the large Daimler CD650 10.6-litre engine and had a five-speed preselective gearbox and fluid flywheel transmission, as well as a 16 ft 4 in. wheelbase. 42 was destroyed by fire before it could be renumbered 442. (D. R. Harvey Collection)

## 51 (DD-72-31)

*Below*: The second batch of six Daimler Freeline D650HSs, numbered 46–51, had Dalfa B36D bodies which were a little more stylish than the Estrela ones. Numerically they followed directly on from the 39–45 class, with the first three arriving in August 1955 and the second trio, which had a one less seating capacity, in September 1957. 51 (DD-72-31) was new in October 1957 and was later renumbered 451 before being finally withdrawn in May 1975. (D. R. Harvey Collection)

## 202 (HH-32-22)

*Above*: Oporto bought ten AEC Regent Vs in the summer of 1960 which were originally numbered 62–71 and were all renumbered 201–210 in 1966. They had UTIC H36/31F bodywork, which was subtly different from the bodies on the many Lisbon Regent Vs, especially in the design around the area of the upper saloon front window. Still in its original livery and carrying an advertisement for MUTUALIDADE pension schemes, 202 (HH-32-22), the second bus in the batch, is travelling into the Praça da Liberdade. (D. R. Harvey Collection)

## 67 (GF-55-64)

*Below*: Before it was renumbered 206, this AEC Regent V D2LA was numbered 67 (GF-55-64). It had a UTIC H36/31F body and entered service in August 1960. It is standing in the Praça da Liberdade and clearly shows the thinner front corner pillars in the upper saloon. The only other Portuguese Regent Vs that had this design feature were those supplied to J. C. Soares of Guimaraes, although these uniquely had every saloon window in each deck fitted with deep sliding windows. The buses had guttering strips over the saloon windows, which also had 'third'-drop ventilators. (D. R. Harvey Collection)

# 3. Leyland Royal Tiger Worldmaster Single-Deckers

### 57 (HI-89-08)

*Above*: Parked on the quayside in Vila Nova da Gaia with the River Douro behind it is STCP 57 (HI-89-08), a Leyland LERT1/1 with a Dalfa B36D body. The Leyland Royal Tiger Worldmaster was a mid-underfloor-engined chassis manufactured by Leyland between 1954 and 1979. A Leyland O.680H horizontal engine was mounted at the middle of the 20-foot-long wheelbased heavyweight chassis frame, driving through a pneumocyclic semi-automatic gearbox. These buses were originally numbered 52–61 and were later renumbered with '400' being added to the existing fleet number. All were delivered in the summer of 1960 and in 1967 were augmented by Worldmasters 62–106, this time bodied by Caetano. Behind the bus, straddling the River Douro, is the double-deck Dom Luís I bridge linking Vila Nova da Gaia to the city of Oporto on the distant bank. (D. R. Harvey Collection)

### 458 (HI-90-12)

*Below*: After withdrawal in July 1975, 458 (HI-90-12) was used as a service vehicle by STCP for over ten years. Standing in Bon Fim Garage yard on 17 August 1990, 458 is a Leyland Royal Tiger Worldmaster LERT1/1 which has had its Dalfa-built chassis rebuilt with completely new front and rear ends. This left the saloon section in its original condition with doors at the front and rear of the bus. The lower front apron has been cut away to reveal a towing hook used to shunt trolleybuses as well as other disabled motorbuses around the garage. (D. R. Harvey)

## 459 (HI-89-09)

*Above*: 459 (HI-89-09) is parked in Areosa Garage yard in 1985. The Dalfa B36D body on this 1960 Leyland Royal Tiger Worldmaster LERT1/1 is virtually in as-built condition, although the driver's windscreen has been rebuilt, losing its lower opening section. The bodywork design with a front entrance and rear exit doors was rather spoilt by having nine small saloon side windows. Formerly numbered 59, it was withdrawn in May 1983, being used by STCP as a non-PSV. (D. R. Harvey)

## 462 (SN-30-24)

*Below*: Many of the Caetano-bodied Leyland Royal Tiger Worldmaster LERT1/1s were rebodied by UTIC with a B38D seating layout and two doors, but this time with the exit in the centre of the body. Parked in Carmo Square in August 1988 is 462 (SN-30-24), formerly 62, built in April 1967 as the first in the batch of forty-five Worldmasters delivered over the next seven months. It was withdrawn in 1995 and sold to the Oporto fire brigade. (D. R. Harvey)

### 463 (SN-30-25)

*Above*: Climbing the hill over the stone sets and tram tracks in Bandeira, near the famous O'Brasilia coffee house, in August 1988 is 463 (SN-30-25). Three years before, in 1985, this bus was carrying the same advertisements. These 1967-vintage Leyland Royal Tiger Worldmaster LERT1/1s had replacement UTIC B29D bodies which also had the capacity for twenty more legal standees, though the reality was that they frequently carried a lot more, especially in the peak periods. (D. R. Harvey)

### 470 (SN-36-57)

*Below*: Leaving Bonfim Garage is 470 (SN-36-57), a UTIC-rebodied thirty-eight-seater Leyland LERT1/1 Worldmaster. It was on gradients like this that the Leyland 0680H 11.1-litre engine came into its own. The climb up the steep hill was because the garage was split on two levels and with the single-deckers housed there, it was necessary to climb through one of Oporto's many village-like suburbs in order to reach the main road where the upper level was located. (D. R. Harvey)

### 477 (SN-41-05)

*Above*: Travelling down the steep hill in the Rua de Sa de Bandeira on its way to the terminus in Batalha is 477 (SN-41-05). It is August 1988 and this UTIC-rebodied Leyland Royal Tiger Worldmaster is working on the 22 route. These rebodied buses had a B33D arrangement and had rather deep saloon windows and large sliding ventilators that were much better suited to the hot summers than the original Caetano bodies. The rebodied Worldmasters remained in service until 1995. (D. R. Harvey)

### 483 (SN-43-02)

*Below*: Still with its original Salvador Caetano body, 483 (SN-43-02), a Leyland Royal Tiger Worldmaster LERT1/1, travels down a sharp gradient on the shop-lined Rua Monsinho da Silveira during August 1984. It is working on the 15 service to Alfandega and is on its way towards the quayside of the River Douro near to the Dom Luís I Bridge. This two-door bus, formerly numbered 83, had been built with a B38D seating layout but had been reseated to a thirty-seater with room for more standee passengers. Although in pristine condition, it would only have another two years of service left. (D. R. Harvey)

**498 (SN-68-20)**

*Above*: Lined up in the lower parking area at Bonfim Garage in August 1985 are two of the Caetano-bodied Leyland Royal Tiger Worldmaster LERT1/1s. On the right is 498 (SN-68-20), with 476 (SN-41-06) next to it. By way of contrast is 484 (SN-46-73), one of the UTIC-rebodied Worldmaster single-deckers, which in April 1980 were some of the only buses in Portugal rebodied with this late body design with a somewhat 'worried'-looking windscreen. Looking very similar is 813 (OM-16-82), a 1981 Volvo B55-55F but with Camo B33D bodywork. Above and behind the single-deckers is Bonfim Garage's double-decker parking area with both Dalfa and Caetano-bodied Leyland Atlantean LPDR1/1s visible. (D. R. Harvey)

**500 (SN-69-45)**

*Below*: Approaching Bandeira, the centre of Oporto's shopping area, in August 1985 on the 15 route is 500 (SN-69-45) (formerly 100). It is a Leyland Royal Tiger Worldmaster LERT1/1 still with its original stylish-looking Caetano B30D bodywork. 500 entered service in September 1967 and was one of just fourteen of the forty-five in the class that retained these bodies until withdrawal, which in this case occurred in June 1986. (D. R. Harvey)

# 4. The Early Leyland Atlantean Era

### 72 (CE-57-01)
*Above*: An official photograph of the first Leyland Atlantean LPDR1/1, 72 (CE-57-01), the only one completely bodied by Metro-Cammell Carriage & Wagon in Birmingham, though it was assembled in Portugal by Salvador Caetano. This Atlantean chassis was the first left-hand drive version to enter service and entered service with STCP in Oporto in May 1962. It was later renumbered 211 and was not withdrawn until July 1979. 72 was the only Atlantean in the Oporto fleet that had opening windscreen ventilators from new. (STCP)

### 213 (IA-42-34) and 215 (BA-93-84)
*Below*: Parked in the upper area of Bonfim Garage in August 1985 are 215 (BA-93-84) on the right and 213 (IA-42-34), both in the post-1970 orange and white livery. The usual Leyland 0.600 9.8-litre engine was fitted at the rear and these early Oporto Atlantean LPDR1/1s were fitted with the three-piece engine bustle. The Caetano bodies had slightly less deep windows in the upper saloon which gave a subtly more balanced appearance when compared to their antecedents manufactured to the Orion style by MCCW. Originally numbered 76 and 74 when new in May 1962, both buses were to be preserved by STCP after long periods in store after their withdrawal in September 1985. (D. R. Harvey)

**214 (BA-93-01)**

*Above*: 'It's the only way to travel!' A young boy sits on top of the engine shroud while using the engine ventilator slots to act as handholds as he gets a free ride on 214 (BA-93-01). In the time of the Atlanteans, this dangerous practice was quite a common sight in Oporto's city centre and along the Esplanada near to the seventeenth-century Castelo Do Queijo. Translated as the 'Cheese Castle', the fortification is nestled into the rocky shore of the River Douro and was built to defend the estuary. Unlike British double-deckers, the rear upper saloon window was fixed and therefore there was no emergency window. (P. J. Thompson)

**216 (IA-43-88)**

*Below*: Originally numbered 77, 216 (IA-43-88) was one of the first production batch of nine buses, numbered 73–81, of Salvador Caetano-bodied seventy-three-seater front-entrance Leyland Atlantean LPDR1/1s. It was fitted with a Leyland 0.600 9.8-litre engine and a pneumocyclic gearbox on a 16 ft 3 in. wheelbase. Entering service in July 1962, it was renumbered in the mid-1970s. It is in the original green and off-white livery as it travels through the city centre. (PM Photography)

### 220 (IA- 61-23)

*Above*: After having been withdrawn in November 1982, the last of the Leyland Atlantean LPDR1/1s with Caetano H41/32F bodywork, 220 (IA- 61-23), formerly numbered 81, was eventually converted to a café. The bus was driveable but tended to be parked in one spot for days at a time. It is parked at Foz in August 1985 and the nearside was fitted with a canvas awning and a number of tables and chairs. It had been equipped with a bottom-opening windscreen and upper saloon front windows in its last few years of service with STCP. (D. R. Harvey)

### 228 (HD-72-72)

*Below*: Working on the 85 service underneath the trolleybus lines between São Caetano and Santa Eulalia in August 1984 is 228 (HD-72-72), which had entered service in December 1963. This route went through a never-ending ribbon development of early twentieth-century housing mixed with warehouses and small factories. Yet, like the mist rising to reveal a previously unknown beautiful view, the bus services to the eastern suburbs of Oporto quite suddenly emerged into a verdant landscape dominated by viticulture. 228, a Leyland Atlantean LPDR1/1, has an attractively styled Dalfa H41/32F body. This body design shows just how similar this was to the dual-door bodies produced by the company on the fifty Lancia double-decker trolleybuses delivered in 1966. (D. R. Harvey)

## 235 (MR-38-50)

*Above*: Originally numbered between 82 and 111, the thirty Dalfa-bodied Leyland Atlantean LPDR1/1s were numbered 221–250 in 1975. 235 (MR-38-50) is working on the 54 service at the passenger shelters in Carmo on 15 September 1983. The bodywork style was derived from the nine Salvador Caetano bodies mounted on 73 to 81 but the detail of the design, with a slightly 'V'-shaped windscreen, a less flat front profile and deeper upper saloon front windows, as well as having chromed window surrounds, all combined to produce a most pleasing looking bus. (PM Photography)

## 239 (MR-40-35)

*Below*: Pulling away from the 54 route bus stop in the Avenida dos Aliados during August 1985 is Leyland Atlantean LPDR1/1 239 (MR-40-35). The bus has a Dalfa H41/32F body and considering that it is already twenty-two years old, it looks in remarkably fine fettle. The bus is moving to the top of the beautifully laid out dual carriageway where lay, all those years ago, a wonderful snack bar whose main 'foody comestible' was a long bun with spiced, bright red boiled tripe and onions in it. The Portuguese nickname the inhabitants of Oporto as 'the tripe eaters' and these rolls were absolutely magnificent even if they were a slightly odd gastronomic delight. (D. R. Harvey)

## 246 (MR-47-53)

*Above*: In August 1967, Dalfa-bodied 246 (MR-47-53) travels beneath the tram overhead as it heads into Oporto to the Avenida Dos Almada, which was the first large commercial street to be opened outside the city walls in 1761. This Leyland Atlantean LPDR1/1 entered service in December 1964 with the fleet number 108 and remained in service until November 1987. The styling of the Dalfa body design is clearly derived from the Metro-Cammell-bodied prototype 72 (CE-57-02), delivered in May 1962. (R. Symons)

## 247 (MR-47-95)

*Below*: Passing the Infante tram terminus – wherein lurks tramcar 273, one of the CCFP-built 'Bogie Americano' forty-seater trams built in 1927 – is 247 (MR-47-95). This 1963-built Dalfa-bodied Leyland Atlantean LPDR1/1 is about to pass into the Rua Nova do Alfandega on 21 August 1987 when working on the 88 route to Alfândega, where the former customs house, built in 1822, is situated. In front of the bus are the abandoned tram tracks to Praça da Liberdade, which had been used by the 1 tram route on 17 November 1968. (P. J. Thompson)

**250 (MR-50-55)**

Dalfa H41/32F-bodied Leyland Atlantean LPDR1/1 250 (MR-50-55) (formerly 111) had entered service in January 1965 and was the last of the 221–250 class. This Dalfa style of bodywork was the last delivered to Oporto that had bodies derived from British design practice. 250 is travelling through Bandeira in August 1988 and is being used on the 78 route to the nearby Carmo Square. (D. R. Harvey)

## 5. The Final Atlanteans

**252, (MO-67-56)**

Negotiating a narrow back street in Bolhao is 252 (MO-67-56). Delivered as 113 in September 1966, this was the second of this batch of Leyland Atlantean LPDR1/1s numbered from 251 to 340. These buses had Salvador Caetano H49/38F bodywork, the design of which broke away from the previous British-styled double-deckers. They had a strikingly angular looking front-entrance bodywork with railed front and rear saloon side windows. (D. R. Harvey)

## 253 (MO-57-55)

*Above*: Standing at its bus stop in the Avenida dos Aliados in August 1985 is 253 (MO-57-55), a Caetano-bodied Leyland Atlantean LPDR1/1. At the end of the nineteenth century, Porto witnessed a great growth as a finance centre, with many finance-based companies becoming attracted to the city. This transformation also led to the opening of many luxury article shops, refined coffee shops and hotels. Work resumed after the 1910 revolution in Avenida dos Aliados, with buildings designed in a Parisian Beaux Arts style lining this most elegant city centre boulevard. (D. R. Harvey)

## 254 (MO-67-57)

*Below*: Only the first ten of the 1966 batch of Atlanteans were given numbers in the 112–121 series and were quickly renumbered 251–260. The rest of the buses were numbered from 261 onwards from new. 254 (MO-67-57) travels along the Avenida da Liberdade while employed on the 52 service on 17 August 1990. 254 is adorned by a wrap-round advertisement for Grundig electric goods. Advertisements like this on double-deckers proved to be a valuable source of revenue for STCP. (D. R. Harvey)

## 260 (MO-67-54) and 261 (MO-67-55)
*Above*: 260 (MO-67-54) was the last of the Caetano-bodied Leyland Atlantean LPDR1/1s delivered in September 1966 to be numbered in the original double-decker fleet number series; in this case it had been 121. It is approaching the Infante tram terminus on the banks of the River Douro and is about to turn the Rua Nova do Alfandega and travel up the hill in Rua Mousinho de Silveira to get to São Bento and its amazing railway station buildings. Passing it is 261 (MO-67-55), which was the first of these buses to be numbered in the new 200 fleet series. (D. R. Harvey)

## 262 (MO-70-94)
*Below*: Having left the Praça de Batalha at the top of the hill, 262 (MO-70-94) rumbles down the stone setts in the Rua de 31 de Janeiro, passing the arched frontage of the nineteenth-century Banco Borges & Irmão premises. This eighty-seven-seater Leyland Atlantean LPDR1/1 is working on the 15 route to Alfandega. As with many of the streets in the centre of Oporto, the pavements are laid out with a patterned mosaic. Travelling up the hill is a SEAT 127, a supermini produced between 1972 and 1982 and based on the Fiat 127. (D. R. Harvey)

### 264 (MO-71-54) and 269 (MO-72-46)

*Above*: Loading up with passengers in the Rua de Sa da Bandeira near to the Bolhao Market Hall is 264 (MO-71-54). It is working on the 78 service to the Castelo do Queijo alongside the River Douro estuary in August 1985. This bus had entered service in September 1966 and it looks as if all of the eighty-seven-seat capacity of the Caetano body might well be needed. It is being overtaken by another identical Leyland Atlantean LPDR1/1, 269 (MO-72-46), which is being used on the 13 service. (D. R. Harvey)

### 267 (MO-71-96)

*Below*: Turning into Avenida da Boa Vista in the Praça de Gonçalves Zarco is Caetano-bodied Leyland Atlantean LPDR1/1 267 (MO-71-96). In the centre of the square is the large equestrian statue of King John VI, who was king of Portugal from 1816 to 1826, while on the extreme right, on the shores of the Douro Estuary, is the Castelo do Queijo, which was built in the seventeenth century as a defensive site to protect the entrance to the river. (D. R. Harvey)

### 279 (MO-75-60)

*Above*: Passengers get on board Caetano-bodied Leyland Atlantean LPDR1/1 279 (MO-75-60), apparently in the middle of the road. In fact the pavement on the left with the tree planted in it separates the tram tracks on the left leading to the Infante sub-terminus of the 1 tram route. This follows the River Douro on the left to Passeio Alegre in Foz on a 4 ft 8½ in. gauge. The bus, standing in the shadows of the large seventeenth-century Gothic styled São Francisco church, is about to climb the Rua do Infante Dom Henrique on its way to the Praça Da Batalha on the 15 route. (D. R. Harvey)

### 282 (MO-77-37)

*Below*: Working along the Avenida de Montevideu coming from Castelo do Queijo towards Foz is 282 (MO-77-37). On 27 August 1986, this Leyland Atlantean LPDR1/1 fitted with Caetano H49/38F bodywork is working on the 78 route to the Hospital de São João and is running along the riverside road towards the mouth of the River Douro. 282 entered service in November 1966 and would stay in service for nearly twenty-one years. (P. J. Thompson)

## 293 (MO-84-20)

*Above*: Standing alongside the open-air market in Carmo Square is 293 (MO-84-20), a Salvador Caetano-bodied Leyland Atlantean LPDR1/1. Although there were still tramcars operating into Carmo in August 1988, by this time many of the tram services that used the square had been abandoned and bus services were in the ascendency. The driver of this one-man-operated 54 service is taking his well-earned break inside the lower saloon of the bus. (D. R. Harvey)

## 299 (MO-89-13)

*Below*: Near to the São Bento railway station on the 15 route is 299 (MO-89-13). The bus is on its way to the Praça da Batalha when operating on the 15 route in August 1985, having left behind the Praça de Bandeira. This Caetano-bodied double-decker entered service in December 1966 and had the standard H49/38F seating layout. A noticeable design feature of these Atlanteans was their front-mounted radiator to assist the cooling of the large Leyland 0.680 11.1-litre engine. (D. R. Harvey)

**300 (MO-69-17)**
*Above*: Negotiating the huge traffic island at Castelo de Queijo is another of the Leyland Atlantean LPDR1/1s with stylish but somewhat angular Caetano H49/38F bodywork. 300 (MO-69-17) is turning away from the distant River Douro into the Avenida da Boavista on the 88 route to Praça da Boa Vista. Stretching for about 3.4 miles, Avenida da Boavista is the longest avenue in Porto and was part of the 1958 Portuguese Grand Prix circuit. The race was won by Stirling Moss in a Vanwall, who sportingly refuted the Race Marshall's decision to disqualify Mike Hawthorn for supposedly driving up a road in the wrong direction. The decision was reversed and at the end of the season, because of Moss's action, Mike Hawthorn won the World Championship by just one point. (D. R. Harvey)

**303 (MO-39-14)**
*Below*: A rather full 303 (MO-39-14) is being crowbarred full of even more passengers as it stands in the Praça de Dom João I with the headquarters of the Banco Portuguesa behind the bus. It is working on the 78 route in August 1984 before going back to Castelo do Queijo alongside the River Douro estuary. 303, a left-hand drive Caetano-bodied Leyland Atlantean, was the penultimate vehicle from the 251 batch delivered between September 1966 and January 1967. The rest of these double-deckers, starting with 305, recommenced delivery in May 1967 and marked the change from MO to SN registrations. The second batch's delivery was completed with 340 on November 1967. (D. R. Harvey)

**307 (SN-49-06)**

*Above*: Although the STCP bus operation was largely based on British practice, there were exceptions to that rule and this one of them. 307 (SN-49-06) is working on the 78 route to the Hospital de São João in August 1984, but in the course of its duties the Atlantean has run out of fuel. So with passengers still in the lower saloon, the bus is being filled up with diesel at an ordinary petrol station at Castelo do Queijo! (D. R. Harvey)

**313 (SN-58-06)**

*Below*: Leaving Bonfim Garage, 313 (SN-58-06) is a Caetano-bodied Atlantean delivered in August 1967. The larger Leyland 0680H 11.1-litre engine had a power increase useful for climbing the steep hills of Oporto. Here the climb through the old nineteenth-century village-like area was because the garage was located on the side of a steep valley and the main exit was via this almost rural-looking road on the opposite side of the valley. 313 was later to be restored and preserved by STCP. (D. R. Harvey)

### 321 (SN-62-05)

*Above*: Working on the 78 route on 15 September 1983 is Leyland Atlantean LPDR1/1 321 (SN-62-05). These buses had a rather angular appearance about them and were fitted with deep saloon windows with every bay having sliding ventilators, which was most useful in the hot Portuguese summers. This light and airy Caetano body was mounted on the long wheelbase version of the chassis and was fitted with the large Leyland 0680H 11.1-litre engine. It could seat eighty-seven passengers, which was frequently exceeded on this busy service. (PM Photography)

### 322 (SN-62-04)

*Below*: In the busy Carmo Square in August 1988, standing alongside the canvas awnings of the open air market, is 322 (SN-62-04), being operated as a one-man bus. This Caetano-bodied Atlantean will soon load up with passengers when working on the 54 route, but only after the driver, standing inside the bus next to his cab, resumes his seat. Behind 322 is Volvo B58-55F single-decker 724 (OR-67-72), a UTIC B32D-bodied bus dating from January 1977, which after refurbishment at Salvador Caetano's body shops would come back in a B33D format and survive until 2002. The Atlantean, however, would be shortly taken out of service at the end of 1988. (D. R. Harvey)

### 323 (SN-62-30)

*Above*: Approaching Praça de Dom João I in the Rua de São de Bandeira is 323 (SN-62-30). This Caetano-bodied Leyland Atlantean is working on the 78 route in August 1984 and, well-loaded with passengers, is seen arriving in the heart of Oporto's city centre. Behind it is the large 1970s premises owned by the Banco Portuguesa which dominates this corner site at the bottom of the hill and into the adjacent Praça de Dom João I. (D. R. Harvey)

### 325 (SN-63-32)

*Below*: Entering the Praça de Dom João I over the cobbled street surface in August 1984 is Leyland Atlantean LPDR1/1 325 (SN-63-32). Hanging on to the Leyland rear engine bustle are two boys who are rather like strap hangers on a suburban train. At the slightest threat of authority boys like this would jump away from the bus and were gone, mixing in with the passing pedestrians or disappearing down side alleyways. The rear of the Caetano bodywork reveals a less orthodox design than the front of the bus with large upper saloon corner windows and two small side windows in addition to the large rear pane above the engine shroud. (D. R. Harvey)

**329 (SN-70-67)**

*Above*: Leyland Atlantean LPDR1/1 329 (SN-70-67) follows four-wheel tram 134 along the Avenida do Brasil at the Rua do Pradão. The tram is a much rebuilt member of the 120–136 class ordered from J. G. Brill of Philadelphia in April 1909, and had semi-convertible saloon bodies on Brill 21E 7 ft trucks. They had two GE 270 55 hp motors and seating for twenty-three passengers. This riverside road was first developed in the late nineteenth century, linking Infante to the fishing village of Matosinhos by way of Castelo de Queijo. (D. R. Harvey)

**330 (SN-71-42)**

*Below*: Waiting 'for the off' on the return journey to Castelo de Queijo on the 78 route from Carmo Square on 15 September 1983 is 330 (SN-71-42). These Caetano-bodied Leyland Atlantean LPDR1/1s were really very large buses with a high seating capacity of H49/38F plus standees, effectively enabling them to unofficially carry around 110 passengers. 330 seems to have almost all of its seats already taken. The bus wears a large advertisement for EFACEC, which is still an important manufacturer of electrical traction motors through to domestic electrical supplies. (D. R. Harvey)

**338 (SN-76-89)**
Stretching for 3.4 miles, Avenida da Boavista is the longest avenue in Oporto. It is sufficiently long that it was the main straight in the 1958 Portuguese Grand Prix. Avenida da Boavista starts at the Rua da Boavista and passes the old Boa Vista tram depot and the adjacent Boa Vista narrow gauge railway station before heading north-west down a dual carriageway on a continuous gradient to end up at Praça Gonçalves Zarco, known as Castelo do Queijo, where there is a long, sandy tourist beach on the Atlantic Ocean shore. Caetano-bodied Leyland Atlantean LPDR1/1 338 (SN-76-89) travels down the hill towards the River Douro, while coming up the hill travelling towards Boa Vista on the 18 route is tram 143. This was a Brill-built four-wheel tram built in 1910. (P. J. Thompson)

## C. Coimbra

Coimbra, on the east bank of the River Montego, consists of a picturesque lower shopping centre with narrow side streets and alleyways leading off the Rua Ferreira Borges and a higher middle area devoted to the ancient university town, while the higher areas are mainly residential.

A metre-gauge electric tram system was introduced in 1910 by the SMTUC (Servigos Municipalizados de Transportes Urbanos de Coimbra). Five Brill four-wheel semi-convertible trams entered service in 1910 while two more were delivered in 1912. Throughout the 1920s, penny numbers of four-wheeled trams were delivered, while in 1931, three Belgium-built four-wheel trams numbered 16–18 arrived, resembling a shorter version of the Lisbon 280–289 bogie cars.

In February 1947, Coimbra began operating the first trolleybuses in Portugal. This new trolleybus system used mainly British-built trolleybus chassis. It gradually replaced Coimbra's tramway network, which closed in January 1980.

Motorbuses came late to Coimbra and were always in a minority. In 1949, a pair of Daimler CVD6s was bought new while in February 1964 two UTIC H40/33F-bodied AEC Regent Vs were purchased, becoming the only double-deckers to ever operate in the university city. The following year, eight rather neat-looking Leyland Worldmasters with Martins & Caetano B34D bodywork entered service with fleet numbers 13–20. In 1977, Coimbra purchased four Caetano-bodied Leyland Leopard PSU3/4Ls and in April 1973 six AEC Reliance 6U3ZLs entered service with UTIC B37D bodies, thus becoming the last British chassis to enter service with SMC. The bus fleet was considerably smaller than that of the trams and only twenty-three British motorbuses were ever purchased.

## The Bus Fleet

**5 (BI-15-43)**
Although numerically the first of the two Daimler CVD6s delivered to SMC, the municipal operator in Coimbra, 5 (BI-15-43) was in fact the second chassis of the pair. The original Castro Reis FB25D body was replaced during 1965 by a new UTIC FB34D body of a style developed primarily to extend the lives of front-engined vehicles used for bus rather than coach work, although in truth it was a little ungainly in its frontal styling. 5 is parked in the garage yard in 1972. (D. R. Harvey Collection)

**6 (BI-15-43)**

*Above*: The first British motorbuses to operate in Coimbra were a pair of Daimler CVD6s delivered in February 1949. This pair of single-deckers had exposed radiators set into the front apron of the well-proportioned Castro Reis FB25D bodies, which looked longer than their actual 30-foot length. 6 (BI-15-43) was rebodied with a similar-looking Dalfa FB34D body in 1961 and lasted in service until 1974. It is parked in the bus garage yard. (D. R. Harvey Collection)

**7 (IC-23-99)**

*Below*: The solitary 1956-built Leyland Royal Tiger Worldmaster LCRT1/1 in the Coimbra bus fleet was 7 (IC-23-99). This single-decker had a locally built Martins & Caetano B35D body which was remarkably similar to those built by Park Royal in the UK for the Sunbeam MF2B trolleybuses delivered in 1951. It had a Leyland O680H 9.8-litre horizontal engine driving back through a pneumocyclic semi-automatic gearbox. It is approaching the bus station on the service from the Coimbra University campus on 10 August 1966. (D. R. Harvey Collection)

**11 (CL-58-11)**

*Above*: Coimbra only ever had two double-decker buses. These were numbered 11 and 12 in the Coimbra bus fleet and were AEC Regent V D2LAs with UTIC H40/33F bodies new in February 1964. They were painted in a yellow and white livery with a mid-deck grey band and a grey roof and were always kept in tip-top condition. Waiting to start its journey on the 2 route to Adémia, about 2 miles north of the city centre, is 11 (CL-58-11), the first of the pair, wearing a large advertisement for Sandeman Port. (D. R. Harvey Collection)

**12 (DL-58-12)**

*Below*: The pair of AEC Regent V D2LA double-deckers had front domes akin to the ten Oporto Regent Vs that were numbered 201–210. There were also eight D2LAs delivered to Lisbon with the same chassis type, and although they all were obviously left-hand drive, Coimbra's 12 had a chassis number in the same batch as the Lisbon eight. It therefore begs the question whether the pair delivered to Coimbra were part of a D2LA order for ten buses and the chassis of 11–12 were diverted to Coimbra? SMC's 12 (DL-58-12) is working on the 2 route. It too has a between-decks advertisement for Sandeman. This port and brandy maker was founded in 1790 by two Scottish brothers, George and David Sandeman. The advertisement carries the logo of a caped man named Don dressed in a Portuguese student's cape and a wide Spanish hat; this well-known advertising image is to be found throughout Portugal. The bus would be converted to an exhibition unit in the late 1980s, surviving until at least 2006 in this role. (D. R. Harvey Collection)

## 15 (MR 70-54)

*Above*: This bus is working on the 10 route to Portela, about 5 miles south-east of Coimbra on the north bank of the River Mondego. It is passing through Portagem, along the Avenida Emídio Navarro, with the iconic Astoria Hotel behind it and the river beyond the tram tracks on the left. Numbered 15 in the SMC bus fleet, this Leyland Royal Tiger Worldmaster LERT1/1 was bodied by Martins & Caetano with a rather pleasant-looking B34D body in June 1965, but the hammering over Coimbra's cobbled streets rather did it for the body and after barely fifteen years it was replaced in February 1980 with a new, if uninspiringly designed, CAMO B33D body. It was later re-engined with a Volvo unit and was taken out of service in September 1993. (PM Photography)

## 19 (MR-94-40)

*Below*: The modern-looking Caetano two-door B35D bodywork looks very similar to the bodies supplied on Volvo B10M chassis. 19 (MR-94-40) is a 1966 Leyland LERT1/1 Royal Tiger Worldmaster chassis with a Leyland O680H horizontal engine mounted in the middle of the chassis frame and coupled to a pneumocyclic semi-automatic gearbox. 19 was originally fitted with a Martins & Caetano B34D body which had just five large saloon windows. It was rebodied in July 1976 and survived until September 1993 as one of the last British-built chassis operating in Coimbra. (D. R. Harvey Collection)

## 20 (MR-94-94)

*Above*: The original Martins & Caetano B34D bodies were most attractive, but with their large side windows they became something of a maintenance problem. Their life expectancy was therefore much less that that envisaged for the rugged Leyland chassis. As a result, the eight Leyland Royal Tiger Worldmaster LERT1/1 chassis were rebodied in 1980 with 20 (MR-94-94) receiving a new CAMO B33D body. This extended the life of the bus by some thirteen years. The bus is parked alongside the River Montego, on whose banks Coimbra is located. (D. R. Harvey Collection)

## 32 (DN-79-09)

*Below*: Parked at Portagem, Coimbra, on the banks of the River Montego is 32 (DN-79-09), a Leyland Leopard PSU3/4L delivered in January 1968 as one of a batch of four buses fitted with Caetano B33D bodywork. Of the quartet, this one had the shortest life, being withdrawn in 1987. The Leyland Leopard underfloor-engined chassis was not that common for bus work, with the AEC Reliance option being far more popular in Portugal. (PM Photography)

# The Smaller Municipal Operators of British Buses

## D. Aveiro

Aveiro, with a population of over 75,000, is known as 'the Portuguese Venice' due to its system of canals and boats, similar to the Italian city. Located on the Atlantic coast north of Coimbra, Aveiro is an industrial city with an important seaport as well as having many tourist attractions. Aveiro began bus operation in February 1959 with five AEC Reliances with UTIC B32D bodywork and a pair of Leyland Worldmaster LERT1/1s ten years later. Over a period of four years nine AEC Reliances with UTIC B39D bodies were purchased, but subsequently the city purchased mainly Volvo B58s and MANs.

1 (LC-77-23)
Aveiro is a seaside city located between Coimbra and Oporto and only ever purchased sixteen British-built chassis. The first-ever AEC Reliances to enter service in Portugal were five HMU2LA UTIC-bodied examples for Aveiro which had Monocontrol gearboxes. These were numbered 1–5 and were new in September 1958 for the ceremonial route opening some five months later. The city subsequently purchased a pair of Leyland Royal Tiger Worldmasters and nine more Reliances. Appropriately, LC-77-23 is working on the 1 route to Esgueira. (D. R. Harvey Collection)

**3 (LC-77-25)**

*Above*: After being rebodied by Caetano in October 1973, 3 (LC-77-25) looked almost indistinguishable from almost any contemporary Portuguese service bus except for the AEC badge on the front grille below the windscreen. This AEC Reliance HMU2LA entered service in February 1959 with an attractively proportioned UTIC B32D body before that was replaced with this longer body, which had deep sliding ventilators in the saloon. (D. R. Harvey Collection)

**6 (PN-62-62)**

*Below*: Parked in the garage yard during August 1985 in Aveiro is 6 (PN-62-62). This was the first of a pair of Leyland Royal Tiger Worldmaster LERT1/1s which had a brief flowering as one of the better selling British-built chassis during the 1960s. 6 had a Caetano B30D body and entered service in August 1969, with two more seats being added to the bus in June 1971. After these two buses, Aveiro went back to ordering AEC Reliances. (G. Morant)

## 14 (SM-71-34)

*Above*: The final batch of AEC Reliances was numbered 13–16. These were built as AEC Reliance U2076s and were originally fitted with UTIC B43D bodies. 14 (SM-71-34) entered service in February 1976 and was rebodied by CAMO with a B36D layout in April 1991. It is seen near to the lagoon soon after it had received this new, high-line, somewhat angular body. (A. Izatt)

## HH-97-97

*Below*: Although not strictly an operating bus, this British-built chassis was formerly Carris-operated 425 (HH-97-97) and ran in Lisbon from 1961 until 1983. This UTIC-bodied double-decker AEC Regent V finished up as the well-equipped 'autocarrobar' in Aveiro and was still there in 2017. Repainted in all-over red, the bus was parked at the university, but although looking splendid its lower saloon was used by student smokers, which rather spoilt the ambience! (D. R. Harvey Collection)

# E. Barreiro

Barreiro is a riverside town situated on the southern bank of the River Tagus, upstream from Lisbon. With industrial development from the beginning of the twentieth century and the northern terminus of the railway serving the province of Setubal, the town has become almost a residential suburb of Lisbon. The local bus operator was TCB (Serviçoa Municipalizados de Transportes Collectivos do Barreiro), who began operating services in January 1957.

**7 (DD-65-80)**
*Above*: Barreiro's Guy Arab UF 7 (DD-65-80) had a UTIC B36D body built in Lisbon and entered service in October 1957. Other than having a large number of small saloon windows, it still retained the British style of bodywork uncluttered with chrome embellishments. It is seen alongside Barreiro's railway station with 2 (AE-24-64), another Guy Arab LUF that entered service in October 1956, parked in front of it. (D. R. Harvey Collection)

**8 (DD-65-82)**
*Below*: One of the first batch of twelve Guy Arab UFs was 8 (DD-65-82). As with all the Barreiro Guy single-deckers, it was powered by a Gardner 6HLW 8.4-litre underfloor engine mounted between the axles. This increased the seating capacity but made accessing and exiting the bus more difficult because of the high floor level. It is parked at the railway head nearer to the River Tagus ferry in 1971. (A. Johnson)

## 8 (BM-26-07)

*Above*: A late British chassis bought by Barreiro were nine AEC Regal VI U3LAs. 8 (BM-26-07) was delivered in September 1973 and confusingly reused the fleet number 8 used on a Guy Arab UF. Parked on the sea front, it had a B39D body built in Porto by UTIC, which was producing at the time this startlingly uninspired body on most of their buses mounted on underfloor-engined chassis. It was rebodied in 1983 with a Caetano B39D body. (G. Morant)

## 14 (HH-99-13)

*Below*: Standing at the River Tagus ferry and railway station terminus in September 1971 is 14 (HH-99-13). This UTIC-bodied Guy Victory MUF had a Gardner 6HLW underfloor engine and was one of a pair of UTIC bus-bodied vehicles delivered in June 1961. The Victory MUF chassis (Medium Weight Underfloor) was a popular export model and was to remain in service until the spring of 1977, when it was replaced by AEC Reliances. (A. Johnson)

## 27 (LF-78-65)
*Above*: 27 (LF-78-65) was a Guy Victory MUF fitted with the larger and more powerful Gardner 6HLX 10.45-litre underfloor engine. It had a two-door, forty-seater body built by UTIC which, with its deep side saloon windows and windscreen, looked a more modern and practical design. It had entered service with Barreiro in November 1970 and lasted with TCP until the end of 1987, when it was sold to the Escola de Condução Especial a Barreirense as a driver training bus, in which guise it is seen being used in about 1990. (D. R. Harvey Collection)

## 44 (BM-98-78)
*Below*: The AEC Regal VI was an underfloor-engine single-decker bus chassis built by the Southall-based company. The model was unveiled at the 1960 Commercial Motor Show and was intended to be a purely export chassis available in both left and right-hand drive versions. The AEC Regal VI had an 11.3-litre AH690 engine with power-assisted steering and air suspension. 44 (BM-98-78), working on the 8 route near the River Tagus, entered service with a UTIC B35D body in October 1973. It was rebodied with this Salvador Caetano B52D body after just ten years of use. This was the last of the seven buses numbered 38–44, which were assembled in Portugal with the chassis nomenclature U3LA. (D. R. Harvey Collection)

# F. Braga

Braga is a somewhat dispersed urban area extending from the Cávado River to the Este River and is the third largest urban centre in Portugal. Much of its attraction is both theological and architectural and it is the seat of the Primate Archbishop of Portugal and of Hispânia. The municipality of Braga (SMB) began motorbus operation in June 1948 and was taken over in February 1967 by a group of entrepreneurs based in Guimarães known as SOTUBE (Sociedade e Irmão Transport Urbanos de Braga). Despite this long name, the group only inherited six Leyland Tiger PS1s and a pair of AEC Regal 9631As. All eight of these buses had FB34D bodies built in SMB's own workshops, and all were right-hand drive.

**1 (IA-12-72)**
*Above*: Numerically the first motorbus delivered to Braga, being purchased by the then municipally owned operator, was 1 (IA-12-72). This was a Leyland Tiger PS1 whose chassis number revealed that it was constructed in 1946. It was completed by the operator, SMB, with an attractively styled FB34D body and entered service in February 1947. It is still quite new as it isn't fitted with the fleet number roundel mounted on the radiator. (D. R. Harvey Collection)

**2 (FG-12-61)**
*Opposite above*: Of the six Leyland Tiger PS1s, only 2 (FG-12-61) was bodied by José Peixoto, a local coachbuilder. It was actually the first bus to be delivered in Braga in January 1947, but after being taken over SOTUBE had it rebodied with a somewhat deep-saloon windowed design by Martins & Caetano with a FB38D layout. It is parked in front of the bus garage alongside a pair of 1967-vintage CAMO-bodied Volvo B58-55s. (D. R. Harvey Collection)

## 8 (CF-16-23)

*Below*: The plain multi-windowed, full-fronted body on Braga's 8 (CF-16-23) was fitted with a FB35D body built by the operator. There was no mistaking the fleet number of the front-engined buses as it was displayed on the radiator grille within a large circular plate. It is parked in Amandio de Oliveira, the main street in the centre of Braga. These right-hand drive Leyland Tiger PS1s entered service in February 1950 and 8 was withdrawn in November 1971. (A. Johnson)

**9 (TH-13-26)**

Only two left-hand drive AEC Regal III 9631As were ever purchased by Braga. New in October 1951 and equipped with an AEC 9.6-litre engine coupled to a four-speed manual gearbox, 9 (TH-13-26) had an SMB FB29D body built by the operator. It was rebodied with a rather square-looking CAMO FB35D body in May 1971. In this condition it only lasted for another eight years. It is parked outside SOTUBE's bus garage in April 1974. (D. R. Harvey Collection)

# G. Guimarães

Guimarães is a city located in northern Portugal, in the district of Braga. Founded in the ninth century on the site of a Roman settlement, the city is often referred to as the 'birthplace of the Portuguese nationality' because of the Battle of São Mamede, which led to the foundation of the Kingdom of Portugal and which was fought in the vicinity of the city in 1128. This led to the independence of Portugal from Spain and the proclamation in Guimarães of an independent Portugal. For a brief time the city was the capital of Portugal.

The city has many historical sites, boasting the tenth-century Guimarães Castle, the remains of a thirteenth-century defensive wall and the Duke of Braganza's Palace, built between 1420 and 1422. There is a bustling city centre with numerous squares and boulevards laid out in the nineteenth century and a thriving tourist industry.

Bus services in Guimarães began on 1 June 1963, operated by the STCG (Serviços de Transportes da Cidade de Guimarães). Buses from the João Carlos Soares fleet in Guimarães augmented the buses in the municipal fleet by being used on a long-term loan basis. Among the earliest arrivals was a solitary new double-decker, the only

AEC Regent V to be operated in Portugal beyond the main cities of Lisbon, Oporto and Coimbra. Initially six UTIC B36D-bodied AEC Reliance U2003 and U2036 buses were delivered or acquired between 1963 and 1971.

TUG (Transportes Urbanos de Guimarães) succeeded STCG from 1 November 1979, and after the takeover initially remained loyal to British chassis with six more very late UTIC-bodied AEC Reliances and six UTIC-Leyland CSPTL11Rs with B37D bodies being delivered. These were the last British chassis delivered to Guimarães.

**5 (LE-48-74)**
*Above*: The driver of 5 (LE-48-74) stands by the front entrance of his bus in the Almeda de Resistencia, Guimarães, in August 1985. This UTIC-AEC U2006 dated from May 1965 and was taken over from the Soares fleet, where it had been fleet number 27. The bus has been pressed into service with a wooden board over one of the rearmost saloon windows after the glass pane had been broken. With some of the more prestigious shops in Guimarães behind him, no wonder the driver looks 'cheesed off' with a bus with a piece of tatty plywood over a window bay! (D. R. Harvey)

**7 (DC-72-86)**
*Overleaf above*: 7 (DC-72-86) was an AEC Regent V LD2LA with a Lisbon-built UTIC H40/33F body. It was equipped with deep sliding glass ventilators in the saloon. Originally J. C. Soares's 34, it was new in December 1966 and operated as part of the Guimarães fleet by Soares, thus becoming the only municipally owned Regent V to operate in Portugal from new that was not in the Lisbon, Oporto or Coimbra bus fleets. The bus was always immaculately maintained and presented and was subsequently saved for preservation. (D. R. Harvey)

**8 (MO-85-28)**

*Below*: What was surprising about this AEC Reliance U2006 single-decker was that despite its modest length, 8 (MO-85-28) had front, central and rear doors! This greatly reduced its seating capacity to a B22T layout but allowed for large numbers of standee passengers in the UTIC body. It was new to Soares in December 1966 and was returned to it as its fleet number 28 before being rebodied by it with a new, very British-looking, almost BET-styled Mota bus body. It is standing in the bus lane in the Almeda de Resistencia, alongside the main shops in the city centre. (D. R. Harvey)

**15 (MS-18-28)**
*Above*: 15 (MS-18-28), an AEC Reliance 6U3ZL with a UTIC B32D body, dated from 1971. This bus was acquired from A. da Costa Moreira in 1979. It is seen passing the main city centre shops on the north side of Almeda de Resistencia on a very hot day in August 1985. The bus is near to Toural Square, which has the most splendid wavy-patterned mosaic pavements interspersed with the beautifully maintained municipal gardens. (D. R. Harvey)

**21 (GF-55-64)**
*Below*: Formerly numbered 206 in the Oporto bus fleet, this AEC Regent V D2LA was acquired in 1980 by Guimarães when it was twenty years old. Being slightly shorter, with less of a rear overhang than DC-72-86, the UTIC body only had a seating capacity of sixty-seven and had half-drop saloon opening windows. It was purchased by TUG as a short-term measure and had been withdrawn by 1988. (G. Morant)

**11 (OS-22-02)**

*Above*: Parked in Guimarães in August 1985 while owned by TUG is 11 (OS-22-02). This AEC Reliance U2036 6U3ZL was one of the six UTIC B32D-bodied buses delivered in January 1979. It had air suspension and a six-speed ZF manual gearbox coupled to an AEC760 12.47-litre engine. These were built at the very end of AEC Reliance production, and although the bodywork was a little uninspired, these buses were able to compete with the contemporary Volvo B58 chassis from Sweden that were getting a very firm foothold into the Portuguese bus and coach market. (D. R. Harvey)

**27 (TM-67-82)**

*Below*: Passing the prosperous commercial outlets on the other side of the dual carriageway and gardens in Almeda de Resistencia during August 1985 is 1980-vintage 27 (TM-67-82). This AEC Reliance U2076 had a UTIC B35D body and in 1999 was equipped with a Volvo engine. Despite this, 27 only stayed in service for another year. The comparatively low height of the front entrance and rear exit doors almost give the impression that the sliding saloon ventilator windows could be 'standee' windows. (D. R. Harvey)

**9 (SN-94-75)**
*Above*: With a body that was only five months old, this UTIC-rebodied AEC Reliance 6U3ZL was new in January 1968 to STCG. The transformation by having this new B28D body would convince the average passenger that they were riding on a new single-decker. Standing in Almeda de Resistencia in August 1985, the driver of 9 (SN-94-75) is changing the destination display before leaving on another trip to suburban Guimarães. (D. R. Harvey)

**34 (JG-89-14)**
*Below*: Formerly in the fleet of João Carlos Soares, 34 (JG-89-14) had one of the last British single-deck chassis to be introduced in Portugal. This UTIC-Leyland CSPTL11R, based on a Leyland Tiger, had an attractive, modern-looking UTIC B37D body with deep saloon windows and a curved windscreen. The only drawback was that it had a two-step entrance which, albeit better than the high saloon floors of the earlier AEC Reliances, would no doubt reduce the longevity of the bus. It was new in September 1985 and despite its stepped access it was still in service in 2002. (D. R. Harvey Collection)

# H. Nazaré

Nazaré is located on the Atlantic Silver Coast. It was originally a fishing village with clinker-built open boats launched off the beach in order to catch sardines and shellfish. Unusually, it was traditionally the fishermen's wives, in their traditional multi-coloured costumes, who manned the boats. In the mid-twentieth century Nazaré became a popular tourist centre with its picturesque seaside village and long sandy beaches. Due to the offshore underwater topography, Nazaré boasts some of the best surfing in the world with, in suitable conditions, waves of over 80 ft being a regular phenomenon. Nazaré has three distinct neighbourhoods: the Praia is along the tourist beach; Sítio is the old village on the cliff top; and Pederneira is another old hilltop village. Praia and Sítio are linked by the Nazaré funicular railway.

The two former Lisbon CCFL-bodied Leyland Tiger PS1s (ex-129 and 130) were acquired in April 1963 and were operated between the harbour and beach up to the newer clifftop developments in Sítio by the newly formed Serviços Municipalizados da Nazaré (SMN). Only six later British-built buses were ever employed on this taxing bus route, being former RN vehicles.

1 (LA-22-78)
Originally a UTIC-bodied C43D coach, 1 (LA-22-78) was operated by RN as their 4196. This rare semi-chassisless AEC Monocoach MC3LA, fitted with an AEC underfloor 6.754-litre engine, entered service in 1987 with SMN. It was rebodied for a third time with this UTIC B37D body in July 1989 and survived until 1997. It is parked by the bus garage near to the Praia. (D. R. Harvey Collection)

**IH-38-36**
This UTIC-AEC U2020 was new in April 1971 to Claras Transportes of Torres Novas, whose fleet was taken over by Rodoviária Nacional (RN) after the co-ordination of rural and regional bus and coach services after the 1974 revolution. IH-38-36, with its UTIC B33D body, was one such vehicle and became 4583 in the RN fleet. In 1990 it was acquired by SMN, who continued to operate the bus until 1997. (D. R. Harvey Collection)

# I. Évora

The first bus services run by SME (Serviços Municipalizados de Évora) inland to the south-east of Portugal began in 1959. From then until 1972, when the municipal bus services were sold to J. C. Belo, an independent operator based in Setubal, Évora only purchased nine British-built chassis.

**6 (BL-29-70)**
6 (BL-29-70) was a Leyland Royal Tiger Worldmaster LRTC1/2 dating from April 1961. It was fitted with a Martins & Caetano B40D body. It was later sold to RN as its 8037 after it was withdrawn in 1972, but had operated throughout the tenure of bus operation by J. C. Belo. The bodywork was a clean-lined design, though slightly spoilt by the multi-windows in the saloon. This bus had rather comfortable coach-style seating. It is lying over in the centre of Évora. (A. Johnson)

**7 (CE-51-87)**
Something of a rarity in Portugal, this was Evora's 7 (CE-51-87). It was a Bedford SB8 with a
B19D body built by Dalfa, who had not long embarked on a change of manufacturing policy by
introducing bus building to their panel van portfolio. Noticeable was the short rear overhang on
the body. 7 entered service in September 1961. It was followed two years later by 8 (HD-31-64),
a Bedford SB13 with a larger UTIC B27D body. (D. R. Harvey Collection)

## J. Stagecoach

The name of Rodoviária de Lisboa became Stagecoach Portugal in 1995. Stagecoach
Portugal ran 135 vehicles on services around Sintra, Oeiras and Cascais, serving
the area to the west of Lisbon. After several years of industrial relations issues and
loss-making, in June 2001 Stagecoach announced the sale of their Portuguese
operations to ScottURB for £14 million.

**602 (23-73-MV)**
New to Stagecoach Portugal in 1999 was ScottURB 602 (23-73-MV), a Dennis Dart with a
Camo B31D body. In October 2005, this bus is operating near to the casino in Estoril, near
to the bus station, when working on the 419 route. Estoril is a rather luxurious tourist resort on
the Portuguese Riviera on the north side of the River Tagus and is famous for its long beaches
and the Portuguese Formula One Grand Prix. Stagecoach purchased eight of these Dennis Dart
single-deckers, which were quickly sold to ScottURB when barely two years old. (A. E. Hall)

### 605 (23-75-MV)

*Above*: In October 2005 605 (23-75-MV) waits in the rain at the bus shelters in Oeiras near to the Estoril railway station. It is working on the 471 service and is one of the eight longer Camo-bodied Dennis Dart SLFs bought in March 1999. All these buses were sold to ScottURB in 2001 after Stagecoach withdrew from its operations in Portugal. Stagecoach operated some 160 Scania L113s, mainly with MPO B37D bodies, so Dennis Darts were in something of a minority during its brief sojourn operating buses on the north side of the Tagus Estuary. (A. E. Hall)

### 651 (08-08-NS)

*Below*: Stagecoach purchased just two short-length Dennis Dart SLFs and 651 (08-08-NS) is the first of this pair. It had a Camo B27D body and began operating in July 1999, becoming one of the last British-built chassis to enter service in Portugal. It is parked in October 2005, near to the bus and railway interchange station in Oeiras, when owned by ScottURB. (A. E. Hall)

# K. British-Built Double-Deck Chassis Elsewhere in Portugal

### 169 (IB-49-12)

*Above*: 169 (IB-49-12) was new to Transul, Laranjeiro, in 1969. As RN 9811, this UTIC-bodied Leyland Atlantean LPDR1A had been converted to an open-top sightseeing vehicle to operate along this part of the Algarve coast. The bus is touting for business on the promenade at Lagoa. Lagoa is one of the most important tourist areas of the Algarve, offering to visitors long sandy beaches, modern tourist accommodation, golf courses and cultural heritage. It is also the centre of the region's wine industry. (A. J. Douglas)

### 62 (EF-49-25)

*Opposite above*: In the district of Setubal, on the south side of the Tagus Estuary, opposite Lisbon, is Cacilha. Here there is a ferry boat connection from Cacilhas to Cais do Sodré in Lisbon. Alongside the ferry terminal is the bus station, wherein is parked Transul's Leyland Atlantean LPDR1A/1 62 (EF-49-25). This Laranjeiro-based operator bought a total of fourteen of these UTIC-bodied double-deckers, with the first five entering service in 1968. This is the second of this batch of buses and was originally numbered 142. The H49/38F body is in its original condition with the front upper saloon pillars being glazed, giving a strange but airy look to the body. In the distance, at sea, there are at least four large ships at anchor at the mouth of the estuary. (D. R. Harvey Collection)

### 46 (BB-33-77)

*Opposite below*: Formerly owned by Belo of Setubal, 46 (BB-33-77) is parked in a garage yard soon after being taken over by RN. Its new ownership is proclaimed by new vinyl RN stickers applied to its bodywork. Rodoviária Nacional (RN) was Portugal's national bus company, operating throughout the country with a range of services ranging from long-distance coachwork to urban and village bus services, many of which were taken over from long-established independent operators after the revolution of 1974. The UTIC H49/39F bodies were mounted on Leyland Atlantean LPDR1A/1s and this somewhat angular body style was unique to the last thirty-five of these left-hand drive double-deck chassis delivered to Portugal. All of them went to four distinct independent operators and survived for an average of about another twelve years. (D. R. Harvey Collection)

### 232 (FA-99-90)

*Above*: The last left-hand drive Leyland Atlantean LPDR1A/1 to enter service was FA-99-90. It was numbered 232 in Eduardo Jorge's fleet based in Amadora, to the north-west of the capital, and arrived in January 1972. It became RN's 5232 after the takeover of Portuguese independent operators with more than sixty vehicles after the 1974 revolution. The RN livery of mainly white bodywork with a yellow bottom skirt was an attempt to give the bus a more modern corporate appearance, but somehow lacked the previous, more distinguished air of the original livery. (D. R. Harvey Collection)

### 171 (IL-58-01)

*Opposite above*: Dumped in a field in Rio Maior, near Lisbon, in August 1988 is 171 (IL-58-01), its green and white paintwork bleached by the hot sun. This UTIC-bodied Leyland Atlantean LPDR1A/1 had been RN's 7711, but had seen better days. It had been new to Transul of Laranjeiro and was the sixth bus of its seven 1969 deliveries. Behind it is LB-29-94, which was withdrawn as RN's 7706, but had been new to Transul as its 167 in 1969. (D. R. Harvey)

### 95 (DG-32-66)

*Opposite below*: Arboricultora, an independent operator based in Canecas, to the north-west of Lisbon, only bought four of the UTIC-bodied Atlantean LPDR1A/1s and they were soon sold to Eduardo Jorge of nearby Amadora, which is also part of the conurbation to the north-west of Lisbon. The bus is about to operate on the 9 service to nearby Odivelas. 95 (DG-32-66) was the third of these buses and dated from 1971. The unusual UTIC bodies built after 1969 had one more seat in the lower saloon than the first five built for Transul. The bodies were characterised by having deep equal-sized windows in each saloon with large sliding ventilators which were echoed in the upper saloon front windows, which unusually opened sideways. By now the body design had evolved and the front dome corner windows were eliminated and replaced by more conventional metal panelling. The windscreen was low-mounted but the heavy-looking sunshade above the windscreen rather detracted from the rest of the body. (D. R. Harvey Collection)

# Tailpiece

The balance of this book is biased towards Lisbon and Oporto, where large fleets of British-built buses were operated. The remaining urban centres frequently started operating British buses after the late 1950s and even then only in small numbers before other European-built buses became readily available. Even Coimbra only ever operated a handful of British-built chassis.

But what a treasure trove!

# Acknowledgements

The author is grateful to the many photographers acknowledged in the text who have contributed to this volume. Special thanks are due to Tony Hall, the late Geoffrey Morant, Phil Moth of PM Photography and Chris Nash, David Packer and Peter Thompson, many of whom were able to research their own archives for photographs and information about locations and dates. Where the photographer is not known, the photographs are credited to my own collection. Special thanks are also due to my wife Diana for her splendid proofreading. The book would not have been possible without the continued encouragement given by Connor Stait and Louis Archad at Amberley Publishing.

# Bibliography

Various PSV Circle O lists of the 1970s.

*Buses*, February 1997, Volume 49 No. 503.

Manning, Ian, *Portuguese, Cities and Municipalities* (DTS Publishing, 2007) – a truly splendid book.

Price, J. H., *The Tramways of Portugal* (LRTL, 1972 and 1982).

Tilly, B., *The Buses of Portugal* (Railmac, 1988).